Robert Lowe Fletcher

The Great Temperance Controversy

Comprising Pearl series of lectures

Robert Lowe Fletcher

The Great Temperance Controversy
Comprising Pearl series of lectures

ISBN/EAN: 9783744751988

Printed in Europe, USA, Canada, Australia, Japan

Cover: Foto ©Thomas Meinert / pixelio.de

More available books at **www.hansebooks.com**

THE GREAT

TEMPERANCE CONTROVERSY;

COMPRISING PEARL SERIES OF LECTURES.

BY

R. L. FLETCHER.

A PLEA FOR THE FALLEN.

A Comprehensive Review of the Various Phases of the Temperance Problem.

INSCRIBED TO

THE WOMAN'S CHRISTIAN TEMPERANCE UNION OF AMERICA.

LOUISVILLE, KY.
PRESS OF JOHN P. MORTON & CO.
1884.

THE GREAT TEMPERANCE CONTROVERSY:

A PLEA FOR THE FALLEN.

PREFACE.

THE deepest problem of the age is the civil, just, and equitable adjust-ment of the liquor traffic, in a way that the mighty stream of human woe springing from this source shall be diminished, and the destruction of human life occasioned by this business shall be prevented. Without undue confidence in my ability to grapple with a subject of such endless complications and great magnitude, I have set my hand to the work of preparing a series of brief lectures, sending them forth as a plea for the drunkard, and as a feeble influ-ence in the work of reclaiming fallen men through the appetite and passion of strong drink.

I have in these lectures viewed the liquor enterprise of America as a carnival of blight and ruin, tending to the ultimate overthrow and destruction of Christian civilization. Its work of desolation moves on at a speed that distances every moral means or influence, by or through which an attempt has been made to cope with the evil. The authentic statistics relating to the rapid increase in magnitude of the manufacture and sale of liquor, as well as to the harrowing moral and physical effects and results of intemperance, tend to dis-sipate every ray of hope for the success and perpetuity of moral culture and religious teaching. However calm and dispassionate men may reason upon this subject, it is certainly true, in the light of statistics, that the liquor demon has subtilely coiled itself in the way, bidding defiance to the progress and ad-vance movment of the Christian enlightenment and moral attainments of the people of our country. [Viewed in the light of the startling increase of intem-perance and the wide range of its field, it is not a fancy or ill-advised belief, that this means will eventually destroy the morality, social happiness, and domestic peace of every home in America. Solemnly impressed with the awful truth of these statements, I have, "first and last," advanced legal Pro-hibition as the only present and future hope for the rescue and reclamation of a race fallen through the captivating power and influence of alcoholic drink. Or, in a word, there is no moral power or influence upon earth capable of restraining or overpowering this giant of destruction. If there is a power among men adequate to this task, it is the mighty arm of a Constitutional Law. On the other hand, if the traffic in ardent spirits is left unrestrained, it bids fair to mar the harmony, if not utterly extinguish, every flame of Christian civilization.

Prohibition is the central thought, aim and objective purpose of the temperance people, and there are grounds for a reasonable hope of success in accomplishing the specific work they have in hand; for it will be, indeed, strange if in the fulness of time in this country, the temperance sentiment of the Christian people, and of the better thinking and acting classes—whether Christian or Infidel—cannot be crystallized into law.

But in the struggle for the suppression of intemperance by legislation, we should not overlook this immediate and practical measure, that the ravages of drink may be restrained and diminished by educating the young relative to the destructive and destroying nature and tendency of alcoholic beverages. Usually the refrain of the drunkard, is that he did not know before he acquired the habit of drink, that alcohol is a pernicious and destructive poison. Manifestly, the only remedy for ignorance is education, and the ravages of drink may be tempered by a careful education of the youth of the land, as to its poisonous and ruinous tendency upon the human system. Teach the youth a sentiment of fear, and of abhorrence of the destroying liquid; teach them from childhood to shun it as a human foe—which it is—and the effect will be wholesome.

Political science, however, furnishes a more effectual and permanent solution of this vexed question. Prohibition has become the password and the battle cry, of all who are engaged in the work, or watch the temperance movement with a personal and patriotic interest; and this current of feeling or revolution is growing deeper and stronger with the ages; and even to-day all the combined powers of the opposing league, cannot stay the progress or change the course of this onsweeping tide. There are plausible reasons for encouragement, though the movement that has legal prohibition in view is necessarily slow, as it is cutting a deep channel. The persistent and prolonged efforts of temperance workers, and the earnest, faithful endeavor of humanitarians, of every class to create a public sentiment upon the temperance issue, are marked progressive features of this closing century; and are but index-fingers pointing to the time when the revolt against intemperance will be successful, and its overthrow will be an accomplished fact, and our beloved country shall be redeemed and rescued from the reign of terror, desolation and sorrow that sweeps over its broad domain like billows from the sea of destruction.

In this brief work, I have endeavored to give the reading public a fresh, interesting, though by no means an exhaustive review of the varied and multiform phases of the temperance question; and what I have written, I have written, as my utterances have sprang from an earnest purpose and honest conviction. Seized with an impulse to do temperance work, I have not waited to coin beautiful sentences, or clothe my utterances in language intended to captivate and entrance. I have been too deeply in earnest to indulge in sentiment and avail myself of the embellishment of rhetoric, or the mere graces of speech; but deeply impressed with the solemn character of the temperance issue, as it stands related to man's present and future well being, I have aimed to "speak forth the words of truth and soberness," and advance wise and conservative views respecting its solution; encouraged by the conscientious belief that work done in the interest of temperance is a work that will tell upon the destiny of the race.

Temperance is the greatest moral and political issue that has come down through the centuries, and it is the duty and mission of individual men, tc assist in whatever way they have ability, in its final and complete adjustment, and adjudication. In view of the many extremely favorable opportunities presented for useful work and well directed effort, the responsibility of the temperance people is manifest and becomes very great. And when we recount the woe and suffering that daily spring from this fruitful source, it is not strange that so much is said and done in the name of temperance. Until the day when the sun fails to perform its revolutions, men with humane and Christian impulses, will be found who will champion the interests of temperance and the cause of fallen humanity. The Divine being, who suffers the scourge of intemperance, will alike inspire men to battle against its work of dethronement. Implanted as deep as the emotions of the soul is the earnest and conscientious purpose of the temperance people to fight until the day of victory against this enemy of mankind.

Men will not shut their eyes against the evils of intemperance. And when they have once carefully surveyed its field of carnival and death, they will not sit down and passively fold their hands; but rather an impulse springing from the deepest recesses of the heart will say to them: "Gird on your full armour to fight as against a common foe." One had as well think of standing by and watching the Infinite Hand in its creation and unfolding of a Universe, without awe and wonder, as to think of a Christian philanthropist standing by and watching the ruin and desolation wrought by the tide of intemperance without an impulse and desire to stay the dark, turbulent, onflowing stream.

Let not the arch-enemy of the happiness and well-being of mankind be deceived with the thought that the siege of battle against his armies will fail or be withdrawn until God shall send forth judgment unto victory.

Finally, a victory for temperance is a victory for Christ and the interest of His Kingdom. "This country for Christ" is the motto faith has nailed to its mast. And in the work for its realization the Christian soldier, and the distinctive temperance worker, can join hands. So this work has a two-fold significance, as has well-nigh every work. But let no one be deceived, this great work in none of its bearing is not nearly accomplished yet. Reformers have thrown one single pebble into the expansive ocean of temperance work, and, from the shore of time, are watching with patient solicitude the deepening and ever-widening circle of the waves it has set in motion. But it is more than probable that temperance reformers have formed a misconception of the extent and magnitude of the work yet to be performed. And it is also possible that the work in hand may extend far into the centuries yet to come.

Legal Prohibition is conceived to be the goal in the race of temperance reform. And Prohibition is the objective point of the temperance people in this present age. But it may be reached before the work of temperance reform is completed; for the suppression of intemperance implies the moral reformation and elevation of the race. And here we see blended together into indissoluble relation temperance reform and the upbuilding of Christ's Kingdom. But Prohibition means the capture of the first great citadel of the enemy. And when Prohibition shall have been accomplished, the greatest barrier shall have been broken down and removed in the way of suppressing disorder, lawlessness and crime; and the greatest stride shall have been taken looking to the realization of the Christian motto, "Our country for Christ."

LOUISVILLE, KY., April, 1884.   R. L. F.

INTRODUCTORY CHAPTER.

⊤HE unuttered sentiments of this brief volume were originally intended by the author for the rostrum, rather than for publication. But their publication has been decided upon as the more effectual means of deriving the greatest benefit from them, and the thoughts and views herein contained, are independent of any consideration or purpose, commended alike to the friends and foes of temperance. Personally the Author has but this word to say in writing upon a theme both familiar and threadbare, I have not relied so much upon the power of sentiment and force of language, as upon the earnest statement of facts, in maintaining the truths I have chalenged.

The temperance issue which has been before the people in one form or another for unnumbered centuries, is an issue of solemn interest, and one that enlists the sympathies of humanity; and a literary work that has temperance for its theme needs but a brief introductory chapter; for where the rays of enlightened civilization have fallen, the nature and extent of the dread reign of drunkenness is familiar even to the children of the present generation; and the reason is painfully apparent why books are written upon this subject, and the Christian World as an army with banners is advancing to battle against this foe.

For half a century the social reformers and christian people of this country have been struggling with the question of temperance reform, and devising measures to subdue the devastating evil of drunkenness. Orators of national fame have consecrated their lives to the cause; Ministers have proclaimed from the pulpit the perils of intemperance, and Statesmen have taken the front rank in advocating measures of relief and restraint; and yet in defiant chalenge of these restraining influences, drunkenness and the train of disorders and dreadful consequences that follow in its wake, sweep on with impetuous power and resistence.

The hundreds of gallows erected annually, the crowded prisons, penitentiaries, poor-houses, asylums and criminal docks, tell in solemn cadences the unmistakable fact, that intemperance and the fateful consequences necessarily and always associated with it, is increasing with startling rapidity. The spread of intemperance is ominous and forbidding. It is a black frowning cloud covering the horizon and extending to the zenith in the sky of christian civilization. And it may be said that the light of heaven above the clouds does not penetrate the gloom or break through in rays of cheer and hope.

We would not indulge in mere sentiments, certainly not in sentiment that has no reality corresponding; but the evils of the liquor traffic cannot be measured by words, and is greater than the friends of temperance rightly estimate, and greater than its foes will admit. Its capacity for destruction is unlimited, if all obstructions to it progress are removed from the way. And it is for freedom and right of way that it is contending. With this advantage gained, how swift would be the work of ruin? License and revenue taxation are brakes applied to retard the progress of intemperance, but with these restricting influences in practical operation, intemperance steadily advances, and, viewed alone in the light of statistics, is in a fair way to strand civilization.

Intemperance is an evil that does not abate of itself. The custom of social drinking has a deep and lasting hold upon the present generation of the people of this country; and as a nation of people we are to reap all that is debasing and destructive in this enslaving habit of strong drink. It is a vicious influence that leaves its trace of blight and ruin wherever it goes, as the serpent leaves its trail in the dust. In the realm of domestic and social life it turns happiness into strife, joy into sorrow, love into hatred, peace into anger, and consumes natural affections as an unquenchable fire. Can an evil, with this tendency, be adjusted to society? And can the adjustment be made so complete that the wrong and injury springing from this fruitful source cannot be discovered?

The American saloon brutalizes the American people. It is a Leviathan, whose tread shakes the continent. It has grown to be a monster of such proportions, that it cannot be chained or bound in irons. The arm of the law thrown around it is but a feeble restraint to its work of ruin and of death. If then the American saloon brutalizes the American people, and its range and power of destruction is steadily increasing, What must be done? There can be but one answer to this question. It must be destroyed. The work it is accomplishing is that of the rabid dog or venomous snake. And what do we do with them? Cage them, protect them, put a restraint upon them, to keep them from doing harm? Most certainly we do not. We destroy their lives without pity or remorse. And if the American people are ever to be delivered and rescued from the ravages of the American saloon, the saloon must be put to death. It is out of harmony with the surroundings. It is certainly out of harmony with Christian civilization. It cannot be adjusted to a virtuous society. There are no grounds of compromise upon which Christianity will suffer it to permanently exist, without a well defined opposition. And it is against this opposition the saloon is struggling every day for its permanency and perpetuity.

There is but a faint hope for deliverance from the gross evils of intemperance from any other source than Legal Prohibition. There is a school of philosophers who believe that in the sweep of ages, as the race by evolution rises to a higher plane of intellectual and moral culture, that intemperance, with its endless train of accompanying evils, will gradually disappear—be forgotten, and that the awful dark, and gory scenes of crime perpetrated in its name will be lost to sight in the background. This may or may not be true. Whether true or not, it is a slow and tedious process of eliminating from society a curse that strikes at the hearts and homes of our people, withering and blighting social and domestic virtue and happiness wherever its influence reaches; and no earnest, adventurous philanthropist is likely to subscribe to such a theory, and sit down and passively fold his hands while this result is being worked out.— But on the contrary, when he surveys the desolation and crime wrought by intemperance, he will feel an impulse to lay hold with all his moral strength of the destroying demon and strangle it to death.

The temperance people will not temporize in dealing with this issue, but will prosecute the work of reform to a cruel termination. The issue is well defined, and the plan of the campaign has been mapped out. Its is a warfare in which the temperance people are in earnest. They have stood by and viewed as it were the field of carnage, where intemperance has done its work and left the field strewn with the slain, and then they have advanced to tenderly care for the wounded and bury the dead. Having thus been brought into contact with this power of darkness and fell destroyer, they know with assurance something of the nature and extent of the ruin that has been wrought. And, supplied with this knowledge, they have armed themselves with logical and forcible arguments, and are hurling these shafts of destruction at their enemy; thundering into the ears of the world the awful truth that liquor is a scourge, and that it is destroying more men than all the pestilences and wars of earth, pleading in the name of God and of humanity that this blighting curse be eliminated from the domain of Christendom, and relegated to the realms of eternal darkness.

The enemies of all that is good have felt the shattering force and power of these shafts, and have in defense, held up an attenuated shield to cover their heart in the day of battle. In extenuation of their criminal business they have framed numerous excuses as reasons for its perpetuation. Those excuses are varied, multiform, disproportionate and irrational. For there is no valid excuse for the existence or perpetuation of the liquor traffic.

In this connection we will notice two of their arguments. Their first article of vindication, is an appeal that a person should be unmolested in the liberty to eat and drink whatever he pleases. This particular phase of argument they are pleased to call personal liberty. But personal liberty when used in connection with rum dealing is a misnomer, and but another name for license—license for brawling, rapine and murder. For these are but the legitimate fruits of the deadly traffic. And when we license the traffic, we license all these, and everything done in the name of strong drink.

The second article of vindication or justification we will notice, is the dismal plea of "Revenue" in the interest of the National Government. This plea—no more than the first mentioned—is not valid. The interest of the Government is in no way subserved, at least it is in no sense dependent upon money derived from this source. This mercenary plea is the lowest and crudest order of evidence sustaining the right of men to manufacture and sell an inflaming liquid poison, that produces insanity and death, and lies at the origin of almost every shade and character of crime. There is not in all the range and realm of thought to be found one valid argument sustaining the worse than pagan idea, that revenue is a panacea for all the ills and woes springing from this awful liquor traffic in the fair land of America.

The various phases of the temperance controversy, at least those most deeply fraught with interest, have been discussed in the following lectures. It is our purpose in this chapter to briefly define the work the temperance people, propose to accomplish, and to speak a word of praise in behalf of men and women who have consecrated their lives to this divine mission of reclaiming fallen men.

The people of this country have been generous in their support and advocacy of temperance principles. But this feature is one of the distinguishing characteristics of the race and age to which we belong. No moral reform in this country, if provided with capable leaders, will ever suffer for a following. Leadership in the temperance campaign is an important factor. No army is likely to succeed without competent Generals. The temperance sentiment of the people will take care of itself, but if an organized effort is to be made to secure a National victory, it must be under capable leadership. Perhaps the peril of the hour is that, of leaders with explosive and dangerous theories that imperil rather than advance the interests of temperance reform. But when the crisis in the conflict comes, doubtless there can be found Generals who can marshal the temperance army and lead it forth to victory. As to temperace sentiment; even bad leadership will not impede its progress. It is a thing that does not grow under leadership; but rather under the resplendent sunlight of Christian civilization.

From the rank and file, of the unnumbered hosts of temperance workers, there will come forth leaders with wisdom, prudence and courage, to point the way to decisive and illustrious victory. And when the men and the hour have met,—the victory won—they will be crowned with honors well earned.

The temperance people have not been unfortunate in the men they have chosen to lead them in their eventful reform movement. In the front ranks, there stands men to-day, whose influence have been a tower of strength, and whose names will be ineffacebly written upon the pages of history. It is not necessary to herald their names, or sound their praise, but to its wise, courageous and manful defenders the friends of temperance owe the tribute of grateful rememberance.

To the Christian temperance women of America, as well as to the men, is due the tribute of praise for duties faithfully done and honors well earned. In defense of the temperance principles, so sacred to every Christian and philanthropist, they have exhibited before the world a degree of devotion, courage and heroism of which they have hitherto been thought incapable. To the labor of their hands, to the wisdom of their counsel, and to the consecrated talent they have brought to the work is largely due every success achieved in the work of temperance reform. They have gone forth to their mission, not heralding resounding theories, but conscious of the solemn character of the work to be performed, have with an earnest, yet dispassionate zeal defined their position, defended their rights, and plead their cause before the world, eliciting the plaudits of a generous and admiring people. Having, not alone through their public addresses and lectures, but through their printed tracts and books, won the heads and hearts of the populace. And it cannot be amiss to say that in their literature it is not so much the force of logic and grandeur of thought that has swayed the multitude as it is the knowledge of the fact that back of what is said or written is the gentle impulses and loving heart of a woman.

Intemperance affects deeply the interest, welfare, and happiness of womankind, and moves deeply the emotions of her gentle, susceptible and loving nature. Beneath the wreck and ruin of the rum haunt, is the sensitive heart of woman; the weight of the clinking glasses, wine casks, and whisky barrels, crushing out its very life. Thus prostrate and overwhelmed with sorrow, deeper than the "Savior's passion in Gethsemane," she hears a voice from heaven attesting the love and presence of God, saying: "Arise, and in my strength struggle against the oppression that enslaves and chains in eternal darkness the souls of men." And unto this heavenly call she has not been disobedient.

How peculiarly, strangely and sadly does the work of preaching the gospel of temperance belong to women. Newspapers and politicians say "do not undertake to regulate by statute laws what a man shall eat and drink;" and some ministers of the gospel say, "keep the temperance question and temperance controversy out of the church and out of the domain of religion." Who then but the woman of America shall preach the gospel of reclamation that is to save a race and a nation from the revelry and debauchery of the wine glass and the maddening bowl? It is to this work many of the noblest women of our country have consecrated their lives; and herein lies the strongest encouragement of success, for no enterprise ever chartered can successfully withstand the resistance and opposition of woman. They have set their hands to the work of emancipating the race from the bondage of strong drink and the task will be accomplished. It was a woman who set the chariot wheels of emancipation of human slaves to moving, and they rolled on, and on, until at length they brought to our beloved people, both North and South, a day of universal freedom and peace. Thus, under the blessing of God will it be in the matter of temperance; and when the shackels of rum slavery shall have been struck from the hands and feet of the poor drunkard, our nation of people shall be freemen indeed.

The interests of home stand closely related to the temperance movement. Its success implies the protection and safety of all that is sacred within the precincts of home. Around home clusters all the hallowed interests and association of human life. It is there, if anywhere, we find domestic virtue and purity of heart. It is there we are supposed to find an exalted ideal of manhood and womanhood. Home is woman's inheritance, and it is to protect this sacred legacy she has come forward to the front rank in the temperance army, baring her breast in the day of battle to the Javelin thrusts of a merciless foe; fighting not for the victors crown, wreathed in immortelles, but for the protection of home—her heart's shrine and eternal abiding place.

In this country of freedom and chivalry, political and certain social and professional rights are denied woman, but the sacred right to protect and guard with patient vigilance her home is not denied her, and here upon this shrine has woman lavished every ambition and hope. And yet, despite her tears and prayers which are the bulwarks of defense she erects; and despite the surveilance of God, the subtle intrusion of strong drink into many cherished homes has been felt, as an unbidden, unwelcome and dreaded monster. The temperance associations of America in a very peculiar sense belong to the women. And it is not strange that they take refuge under this sheltering ægis, when the terrors and desolation of rum drinking invade the very sanctity of the domestic circle.

Christian philanthropy and the self-preservation of the race, as well as social and domestic interests, unite to demand the suppression of the liquor traffic. It is for this the brave men and noble women of our fair republic are hoping, working, praying. The struggle for legislative prohibition bids fair to be protracted if not interminable. But the ultimate triumph of temperance principles cannot be questioned. There are discouragements to face; but throughout the whole fabric of National life is woven the golden thread of human progress; and the race is gradually rising toward a higher and nobler estate. The crowning triumph of progressive and enlightened civilization will be to banish forever from its borders the destructive evil of liquor. A union of hands and hearts, concentration of effort and crystallization of sentiment will usher in the millennial day of freedom from the reign of strong drink. In the work yet unfinished, the friends of temperance may encounter difficulties and discouragements that will make the foundation of their faith tremble, but the foundation stones upon which their faith rests will never be shattered or broken up.

The Temperance Controversy.

THE sentiment of the intellectual, moral, and religious people of our nation, well nigh universally, seems to be that the liquor traffic, which has
wrought such frightful devastation and ruin throughout our land, must be prohibited. That element of society whom we cheerfully admit, have the interest
and welfare of our nation and of mankind throughout the world at heart, look
deliberately and calmly upon the ruin that follows in the wake of the manufacture and sale of strong drink, and say from humane and Christian impulses,
that the liquor traffic must be suppressed. This demand is rational, humane,
and just. The people who seek this change or reformation in the affairs of our
nation are actuated by motives to promote and advance the happiness and prosperity of their fellow man morally, intellectually, physically, and in every respect. The motives are pure and worthy. The righteousness of the temperance
cause can not be challenged. The character of its advocates can not be impeached. The sincerity of purpose that animates their course can not be sul-
lied or reproached. The temperance people, in their work, are simply waging
a moral warfare in the interest of those who are incapable of protecting them-
mselves from a destroying foe.

From the attack springs the defense. The drunkard opposes legislation
that threatens the deprivation of the liquid fire he so much craves. The toper
loves his sparkling rum, and will not submit to being deprived of it. The
midnight reveler in the palace hell and guilded haunt of infamy, vice and
lurid crime, says it is an unwarranted infringement upon his right and liberty
as a man and as a citizen, to legislate against the time-honored custom of drinking rum and "kindred spirits." Saloon men say it is a refraction of the Constitution of our government to suppress by the majesty of the law the manufacture and sale of intoxicating drinks and beverages.

The spirit of the Constitution of our government implies perfect liberty
for man, woman and child in all the honorable walks of life. But that liberty
has been misconstrued and abused. Criminals have taken the soft mantle of
liberty and placed it about their shoulders, and claimed it as their protection.
Violators of all that is honorable and just have taken that sacred parchment,
the constitution of our great government, and nonchalently wrapped it about
their corrupt lives, or held it up as a shield to their infamous enterprise, claiming that it afforded invulnerable protection. The men who stand for the defense and protection of the liquor traffic against the assaults of those who would
mercilessly destroy it with one mighty sweep of legislation, deserve a hearing

upon the constitutionality of prohibition. But when we turn to consider the Constitution as touching the great liquor problem, we have to interpret it according to the spirit of that document. There is nothing of a specific or literal character in that instrument of writing, touching the legality of the liquor trade, or in any way controlling, governing or influencing legislation for its prohibition and suppression.

At the time the Constitution of our government was constructed, the liquor traffic in this country was not of such a character or nature as to command attention or demand consideration as an issue of national importance. But I shall always think that the framers of the Constitution should have left blanks in that mighty document for slavery, the liquor traffic, and polygamy —the triple relics that have burdened our nation with woe, with sorrow, and with ruin. And for the remaining two of these blighting evils, constitutional amendments must yet be enacted.

Suppose it is against the spirit of the Constitution of our government to legislate against the rum traffic! Suppose even that a clause in that document specifically declared that such legislation should not be enacted! What then? Would it follow that it is beyond the reach and power of men to change that Constitution? Is the Constitution of our government infallible, unalterable, and unchangeable? You will probably answer "yes," but I answer "no." There is nothing in the affairs of human government infallible and unchangeable, but the eternal principles of justice and right. If in the sweep of ages and of centuries, the perfected Christian civilization of the world demands a Constitution, that thing will be accomplished. If the Constitution of our government did not sanction, or even if it absolutely forbid legislation against strong drink, it would not prove an irresistible barrier to the intentions, designs and purposes of the temperance workers of America. Even that would not turn back the mighty tide of public sentiment which sweeps over the country favoring prohibition.

There is something in this country stronger, abler, and more powerful than the Constitution of our government. That something is public sentiment, public opinion, the will of the people, the voice of the people, the suffrage of the people. If a demand comes from the people to change the Constitution, it will be changed. There is no statute law upon the books of our nation that cannot be changed, modified, or repealed if the voice of the people demands it. Humanity must be sheltered and protected at all hazard and peril. The mistakes of a nation carried down for a century must be changed, corrected, or obliterated when discovered or fully understood.

The union of States, our nation, our government, is older than our Constitution, and they have superior rights to the Constitution. It was Lincoln who declared that the Union was older than the Constitution. It was the Union that made the Constitution. If, as the enlightened civilization of the nineteenth century clears the way, it is discovered that the Constitution of our government is wrong or at fault, or lacking in any respect, think you that the people of this nation will submit to or tolerate that wrong rather than lift their voice in an unanimous appeal to correct that wrong or amend that fault. I believe that the Christian civilization of the twentieth century—which century is not far distant—will set up an ideal standard—at least an infinitely higher, purer, and nobler standard of human government than the one by which we are governed in this day and century. And if the truer and loftier conception of the civilian and statesman in that age demands a changed, an improved, or even a new Constitution for our national government, they will get what they demand, even though it should be purchased by the blood of patriots.

Then away with the cavil that it is unconstitutional to legislate against the vicious and criminal traffic of rum and whisky. The rights of the people are more sacred than the constitution of our government. And if the constitution imposes or inflicts a wrong upon the people, or suffers it to be done, then the Constitution must be altered or amended. If it is unconstitutional to legislate against the liquor traffic, then the Constitution of our government is woefully wrong, and will sooner or later be changed, even if that change must be accompanied by the ruthless tread of soldiers, and the iron heel of war. It is a grander thing to have a country without a Constitution than a Constitution without a country.

There is something more cruel, devastating, and ruinous than the clashing of armed factions in civil conflict or national warfare, and that something is the rum traffic in its hideous deformity and pestilential sweep, as we view it to-day in America and Great Britain. The Christian civilization of the future will demand the abolition of the whisky trade; peaceably, if possible—if not, the traffic will go down before the clash of arms. As other great reforms have been effected by the people of this country, so will the great reform of prohibition be accomplished. We have tried regulating and controlling the liquor traffic by license law, but by general consent or Christian men, of moralists and philanthropists, that is a failure. Under the protection of license the liquor business has increased to alarming proportions. Under the protection of license law the rum traffic has flourished as a green bay tree; or, to change the figure, it has increased in an ever-widening circle, until its dark, billowy tide has flooded our country, carrying ruin and death to every home and household in America?

The sweeping and irresistible increase in proportion and magnitude of the distilling and manufacture of whisky and beer is alarming to contemplate. And the fateful ravages and frightful results springing from their use has been heralded from land to seas, and everywhere, wherever the gleaming sun of civilization sheds its cheering light, the people are familiar and conversant with the devastating and blighting influence and tendency of social drinking and intemperance upon the morals and lives of men, and of society in general.

The magnitude of this destructive evil and pestilential curse is increasing at a ratio that outruns computation. The statistics touching this awful fact are terrifying to read and ponder. All the facts concerning the increase of the liquor trade and its deadly and perilous influence upon society and upon the morals of men are fully known to the people of America. The statistics have been carefully compiled, classified, and laid before the eyes of the people of our country. And those who have not felt the dire evils of intemperance personally, or in their own homes, are familiar with the ravages the bestial rum business is committing.

Familiarity with the solemn and forbidding facts touching the rapid and sweeeping increase and influence of drinking and drunkenness within the bounds of our Nation, has created and given birth to a sentiment of challenge and opposition to the increase and spread of the cruel work of this hideous foe to human happiness and human liberty. Intelligent men view with alarm the steady, progressive increase of the whisky traffic and the results of its use upon men, and, with a candor and earnestness that inspires respect, they challenge the very existence of the whisky traffic as immoral and as a menace to civilization and to our Government. I refer to the wide-spread and universally prevailing sentiment that exists to-day in a truer and more vital sense than it ever existed before—that the manufacture and sale of strong drink, under the laws of our land, must and shall be suppressed. The verdict of the intelligent Christian temperance peope of America to-day is, that the manufacture and sale of whisky and the blighting effect it entails upon humanity cannot be longer endured; and that the laws of our Nation shall be made to forbid and prohibit, rather than foster and protect, this criminal enterprise.— This sentiment is growing stronger, and will eventually prevail and accomplish its designs, and that, too, in the face of a hostile foe and a battling enemy. If the majority of the people of our country agree upon prohibition, they will get prohibition, even if it necessitates breaking and perverting every law of the universe. Constitutional or unconstitutional, prohibition will be accomplished whenever the people heartily and with a meaning demand it. And the hostile opposition of an embittered foe will only hasten the victory of this divinely conceived reform among men.

There was a time in the history of our country when free rum was endured; afterward it became necessary to license the traffic. That marked an epoch, a partial reform. To-day the appeal and the prayer of millions of people rise up for prohibition, for the destruction and eternal banishment of the traffic from the fair, prosperous, and happy land of America. Shall that appeal, that prayer be granted? If not, why not? In America the majority rules. Marshall your hosts to the ballot box and answer that appeal and prayer for yourself. Intemperance is a product of modern civilization.— It has grown up with our country, and is identified with the progress of the nineteenth century. The appalling proportions and magnitude of the manufacture and sale of strong drink has been commensurate with the steady increase of the wealth and prosperity of our nation. This is an age of thrifty enterprise, and the good and the bad, the lofty and debasing have kept pace in their swift stride toward their common goal and common destiny. A crisis comes. The right, the good, the true prevails, the false, the vicious, the criminal perishes in the heat of battle. Intemperance and drunkenness have grown up side by side with Christian civilization, but the fetish breath of the drunkard has become repulsive. The pestilential scourge of inebriacy has become intolerable, and the moral and intellectual elements of society, says this scourge shall be endured no longer. The moral strength and manhood of America is to be tested in the decision of the vitally interesting problem of temperance.

Intemperance has become so universally prevalent, and its results so distressing and heartrending, that it mars, if it does not utterly destroy, the harmony of the Christian civilization of the nineteenth century. Licensing the evil is a moral degradation in itself. The tide of sin that springs and flows from this source can no more be governed and controlled by license than could a gnat upon the bosom of the sea control its waves. And the question paramount in the minds and hearts of the better thinking and acting people of our country to-day is, have we not the moral right and power to prohibit the manufacture and sale of strong drink? It is for the accomplishment of this design that the brave and noble hearted men and women identified with the temperance cause are working. I honor the early workers in the temperance cause, who were animated by this thought, and had this purpose in view, who have hoped against hope, and confronted barriers at once irresistable and overpowering. For, from the beginning until now, Prohibition, and not the ribbons, pledges and gaudy banners of temperance societies, has been the true war cry, and from the twilight of the morning and day of reform, some temperance workers grasped this truth and worked with this puspose in view.— Temperance ribbons and pledges have served some purpose, but their influence and weight have been as fragile as the material of which they are made, in effectually resisting the spread, or suppressing the evils of drink; and in the ratio to which this fact is being realized and understood, the necessity for Prohibition by legislation is finding expression in the minds and actions of men; and henceforth until this question of temperance is settled, Prohibition by legislation will largely command the attention and monopolize the efforts of the royal army of temperance workers.

Temperance societies that have aimed solely at the individual reformation of man by influencing him to abstain from drinking, has and ever will be a conspicuous failure. This is necessarily true from the fact that such means of reformation does not reach the great masses addicted to drink. This means of reformation has no more affected or influenced the great swelling tide and current of intemperance, than would changing the course of some small tributary affect the restless, surging volume of the Mississippi. And yet for thirty and perhaps forty centuries moral suasion and temperance pledges have been the only implements of warfare with which intemperance has been fought. But this startling fact serves no better purpose than to illustrate man's moral blindness. The children of Israel occupied forty years of precious time in crossing the wilderness, when the journey might have been made in two weeks. The world, in the matter of resisting intemperance, has been aimlessly wandering in the wilderness until they have wasted forty years—yea, forty centuries. Solomon, thirty centuries ago, said: "Wine is a mocker, and strong drink is raging, and whosoever is deceived thereby is not wise." We say the same thing to-day of wine and liquor, and we see this awful verity which the wise man uttered illustrated in every day life among us; and humanity will continue to witness these things until the end of time, unless Prohibition by legislation can be accomplished. Prohibition of the manufacture and sale of this raging strong drink is the only thing that will save mankind from the blighting curse, disgrace and sin of drunkenness. Can we accomplish Prohibition? That is the greatest problem the Christian civilization of the nineteenth century has to solve.

The interest of citizenship, the interest of our people individually and collectively, our interest as a people and as a nation, the prosperity and happiness, and, it may be, the perpetuity of our nation and of our institutions of free government depend upon the prohibition of strong drink. And the enlightened sentiment of this Christian age and country demand Prohibition as a restraint to immorality, vice and crime, and as a safeguard to human liberty. And is it possible that the people of our nation cannot check the progress and even destroy that which has been a menace to human happiness and civil liberty. As the years sweep by, the importance and necessity of Prohibition become more and more manifest and imperative. In the light of an advanced Christian sentiment drunkenness becomes more and more intolerable. In the past ages that were mantled with darkness and gloom, the demoralizing tendency of drunkenness and its vicious influence upon society was not apprehended and realized, but as the world grows older, and mankind struggles toward loftier and nobler attainments, it feels more sensibly this mighty burden impeding its progress.

If the Christian civilization of this age could endure the obloquy, shame and ruin, that intemperance inflicts upon our Nation, it certainly would spare the rum drinkers the humiliation of depriving him of his distillery and his dram-shop. But men of moral sentiments and philanthropic impulses chafe under this disgrace. As intemperance increases, growing year by year more vicious in its character, Christian men and women become more and more pronounced in their determination to destroy this evil! to crush this boulder and clear the way for an untrammelled progress and advanced civilization.— License cannot be made strong enough to prevail against the spread of intemperance. And Prohibition seems inevitably and imperatively necessary. Our Christian civilization cannot be purified and advanced until this great moral reform is accomplished. Toward this glad consummation we are looking forward with mingled hope and expectation. But before discussing the necessity and prospects of Prohibition as a national measure, we wish to say a word about license and the license system in explanation of it, and if you wish to so construe our remarks—in defense of it.

Our people have been fretting and chafing about licensing the manufacture and sale of liquor in all its varied forms, and have hurled the shafts of censure indiscriminately at the men who enacted or suffered the license law to be enacted. But it is marked stupidity and drollery to censure the license law by which our government has sought to control the sale of strong drink, and especially is it supreme folly to censure the Legislators and Representatives of our Nation for enacting such a law. Fair reasoning, and an analysis of the facts, will clearly evince the truthfulness of this statement, broad though it may seem. As we have said before in substance,—our country began with the free manufacture, sale and use of rum. One century ago,—and we may limit it to half a century, there was no public sentiment or public opinion or agitation favoring the suppression of the liquor traffic as it existed then within a limited and narrow compass, compared with the sweeping range and compass of the blighting traffic to-day. Gradually, but we may say swiftly—as swiftly as the distilling, sale and use of intoxicating beverages has increased, and drunkenness has spread,—just so swiftly has an universally prevailing sentiment and public opinion favoring the suppression of this accursed enterprise, grown up and matured. If there ever was a time when the manufacture of Whiskey, distilled from corn, could have been mildly and peaceably suppressed, it should have been done by all means. But at that age of the worlds history when such a thing was possible, the people could have known the destructive and debasing effects of Whiskey only by moral intuition. And history goes to show that our forefathers, and honored ancestors did not have a very great deal of foresight or moral iutuition. They either could not see, or else they did not take a look down the centuries, to see what the effects of intemperance would be upon the succeeding generations of their childrens children. The liquor traffic, when our ancestors, one or two or three generations in the past—had to deal with it, was in an undeveloped or embryo state. But little did the people of half a century ago think that the manufacture and sale of Whiskey, then a comparatively harmless, obscure and insignificant business, would develop into a business of such giant proportions, carrying dismay, blight and ruin to well nigh every household of America, convulsing the civilized world with terror, sweeping millions of strong men and women before it into the vortex of death, distancing in its wake of ruin, the scourge of pestilence, and ravages of war.

Strong drink was always ruinous and blighting to civilization, but the traffic of strong drink, and the effects of intemperance to-day is not what it was fifty years ago. Then its use was common, and approved we may say—by all. But with the advance of thought, of culture and of civilization, it has developed in giant proportions, and to-day threatens the very existence of Christian civilization. When the formidable character of this destructive traffic was unknown, there was no opposition to its use, and consequently it was not legislated against, when such legislation was possible. And now after we have come to realize and understand fully the true character of this blighting evil, we find it practically impossible to legislate against it. In the transition or progress from bad to worse, when the people began to realize the power of liquor to harm and to destroy, they done that which alone, they had power to do, that was to seek to limit and to curb the swift increasing evil, by imposing a license upon the manufacture and sale of liquor. It was an attempt at reform in an age when the character of true reformation was not understood or appreciated by the people, and when a truer and higher order of reformation was practically impossible. And let me tell you, that there never was and never has been a day within the history of our country and within the age of the world, when the nations of the earth, singly or collectively, had it within their grasp and within their power to literally eradicate and banish intemperance, and the means of intemperance, by sufferage, by legislation, or by the iron decree of despotism. We are to-day approaching as near the consummation of this great moral reformation as any people or any nation of the world ever approached, and we will need twenty-five years yet to complete the herculean task. I consider the license law a step toward this higher and truer reformation, namely, Prohibition. I honor the statesmen who, when they discovered that they had it intheir power to curb the ravages of intemperance by licensing the manufacture and traffic of strong drink, for exercising that power. For there never was a time when they had the power to do more than this. There never has been a time when the representatives of our people who favored Prohibition, either in the Legislature of our States or in Congress, had a majority enabling them to pass prohibitory measures.

There never has been a time when the constituents of our representatives and legislators have urged the necessity and importance of Prohibition in a way to make their influence felt. Statesmen are powerless to do those things which their constituents do not recommend, or which they openly oppose. Or, in other words, to make it plain, a statesman elected by temperance voters will favor Prohibition; a statesman elected by a rum-drinking community will vote against Prohibition. And it is evident that the power to accomplish Prohibition lies with the people, the individual voter and suffragist.

In the first place we have got to work for a majority of voters among the people, and at the ballot-box, favoring Prohibition; then Prohibition is within our grasp, and not before. But we have not yet reached this day of possibilities. Then do people complain, that in the imergency of our inability to accomplish Prohibition, that we should avail ourselves of the license law.— Who would favor removing the license from the saloon and the tax from the distillery, unless we had a statute-law upon our books prohibiting the manufacture and sale of whisky? Who does not know that in the absence of a prohibitory law, removing the license law floods the country with free rum? And yet the license law, which stands between the people and free rum, is the very thing the people, in a maddening frenzy, have cried out against, anathamatizing those statesmen who were so morally corrupt and depraved as to license and legalize the distilling and traffic of rum and whisky. Look at this thing in a national light. It would have been better to have prohibited the manufacture and use of whisky, instead of licensing its manufacture and sale. That is conceded. But the counsels of our nation never had the power to prohibit and to banish this traffic, but the restrained the accursed traffic by licensing it. Now the question is a fair one: Which is preferable—the license which the provided, or free rum? We will not discuss this question further, but will leave it with you to answer. The great moral problem pressing upon the minds and consciences of intelligent and right thinking men is, can we effect Prohibition? Can we enact a national law suppressing the distillery and saloons, and forbidding the foreign importation of intoxicating liquors?

The temperance man generally says, yes, to this question. But the man who drinks, whoever he is, and wherever you may find him, says no; and that with an air of gusto and bravado. And, to be candid, the question of Prohibition is a question for the future to answer, a problem to be solved in the ages to come. There are many who ardently say that in a few years we will be able to accomplish this masterly reform. As for myself individually, while I have the moral courage to fight in this battle of reform, I confess I do not anticipate a swift or speedy victory over our enemy. I can give a reason for the faith that is in me, in cherishing hope, and in using my humble talent in a work that has for its purpose the annihilation and utter extinction of the manufacture and sale of ruinous drink throughout the broad domain of America; but

I cannot tell you how quickly that cherished object will be accomplished.— Would to God that we could to-day, or upon the coming morrow open all the whisky flasks and rum barrels and empty their contents into the rivers, that the lurid, flaming beverages of hell and destruction might be floated down into the surging gulf and fathomless sea. It would be better for it to float down to the ocean via the Mississippi than for it to float down into men's stomachs, to burn up digestion, to heat the blood, to fire the passions, to madden the brain, inciting murder, incendiarism, adultery, and every kind of crime that lurks in the human heart. But moral reforms come slow, traveling along sometimes at a dying pace; yet, we remember that while the mills of the gods grind slow, they grind exceedingly fine. The destruction of the whisky traffic bides its time, that time may be delayed, but as God reigns, this accursed traffic will be trampled in the dust by a conquering host. The reclamation of mankind from drunkenness and the banishment of the liquor trade are events intimately linked and interwoven with the fate and destiny of our Christian civilization. If Christian civilization goes forward, this great moral reformation will be accomplished in the near future. If Christian civilization shall take a retrograde movement we may bid farewell to this tenderly nestled object, which has become the cherished idol of every noble heart and life.— With mingled hope and fear thinking men touch this problem, whose solution lies as deeply buried in doubt as the rocks lie buried in the bottom of the sea.

It is only as you link the great temperance problem with the progress of Christian civilization that you get ground upon which to plant your feet. It is a conquest in which the religion of Christ has got to bear the brunt of battle. Some people are cherishing the thought that this great work is pretty nearly accomplished. But not so. This is the eve of battle. To-morrow the hard fighting must be done. I tell you that by the slow, steadfast process of evolution the standard of moral and intellectual culture among our people must be raised before intemperance, and the means of intemperance, can be banished from our land. If we are waiting for anything, we are waiting for this. They ask, why do we not accomplish Prohibition to-morrow? You say you can accomplish Prohibition. The answer comes back, we are waiting for the dissemination of religious truth, for the enlightenment of the race. We are waiting for the conquests of the school and the sanctuary. In the near future, when men shall have been better educated, and greater numbers of our people shall have been converted to the truths of divine revelation and to a holier life, then we will have the moral courage and moral strength to cope with this giant evil and destroy it. And this is just as near as we can come to the solution of the temperance problem. Yo cannot cross a stream before you get to it. You can not pass prohibitary laws until you have got a majority at the ballot box and in the legislative halls favoring it. The ballot is in the hands of the ignorant and corrupt, as well as in the hands of the educated. The majority rules. We want Prohibition, but it is voted down. What can be done? Work upon the lives and morals of the men who voted it down. Educate and Christianize them. If this fails, then our issue and our people are lost, and that eternally.

But men of courage are not apprehensive of such results. It is not a blind faith in us to repose a trust in our ability to cope with and overcome the blighting evils of intemperance. Our faith rests upon the triumph and vindication of the eternal principles of right, justice and truth. Our hope is built like a colossal tower upon these foundation principles of human government, and, when wisely reviewed, it becomes a matter of destiny that our efforts to suppress intemperance shall be crowned with illustrious victory. Not a chance, fate or destiny, which may or may not be rerlized, but a destiny that stands related to the principles involved as cause stands related to effect. Reliance upon sheer fate is a delusion. Napoleon believed in fate, and that he was a man of destiny, but the great General lived to see his sun go down in the darkest night. The eternal principles of justice and truth are destined to triumph. It is in this sense that I use the word destiny, and it is in this sense that fate or destiny will control the results in the protracted war of temperance and sobriety against the rum traffic.

Christian civilization is the stone that is to eventually crush and grind to dust the evils that haunt our land and burden our nation; and the liquor traffic will yet share the fate of slavery and kindred evils that have trammelled the progress and advancement of this glowing age. If we lack in faith in the Chrissian religion and in the influence of education upon the masses and the humanizing power of each of these forces upon the conscience, the heart and the intellect, than singularly dim and frail must be our faith in our ability to remove the wide spread scourge of intemperance. But if our faith is strong in education and religion and their humanizing influence upon the mind and hearts of men, then correspondingly firm and settled will be our confidence in the successful issue of this great temperance campaign. Those of us who believe in God, in the church of God and in the truth of divine revelation, look forward with bright hopes to the time when the religion of our blessed Lord and Saviour shall have completed its conquest over the world, when every knee shall bow, and every tongue confess Christ as the Mesiah, and the Son of the true and living God.

Think you not that when that bright day shall have been revealed and the supremacy of Christ Kingdom shall have been established in every land throughout the world; that then, if not before, we shall have removed from our escutcheon and shield the dark forbidding inscription: "A nation of drunkards." It seems to me dear friends, that the religion of Christ is the only breakwater against the mighty tide of intemperance, that is flooding our nation. It is rock upon which we stand ; if we step from off of it, we will perish in the quicksands of doubt and unbelief.

We cannot effect prohibition by the ballot or by any other means conceivable, unless we can improve our civilization, and we cannot advance our civilization without the power and influence of the gospel of the religion of Christ Jesus. Then where do we stand? We stand upon the Bible. If not, then we have no foundation, but sinking sand. If these are the facts touching this great truth, let us then see to our footing, let us plant our feet upon the eternal rock of ages, and there stand, "and having done all, stand." Let us then improve our education, our religion and our politics. Let us nerve ourselves as against the day of battle, and with these implements of warfare fight the foes of humanity and human government. Let us with these grand principles as foundation stones, thereon erect the fair structure of National government, and after while as ages pass by, we will rebuild the structure of our National temple and Christian civilization upon the ruins of intemperance, and dedicate the consecrated work of our hands to the living God.

A Nation's Shame.

ATIONS, as well as individuals, are often the victim subjects of pride and of shame. As glittering possessions and dazzling achievements fill men with pride and pomp; so eminence of position, or the prestige of a perishing fame, makes nations hauty and imperial. Whatever is true of individuals is largely true of Nations; and the characteristic features that distinguish a Nation characteristic features of its subjects individually. If it is admissible for individuals or for Nations to cherish the feeling or spirit of pride; there are plenty of each, that have just reasons, for the exhibition of such a trait of character. Perhaps there is no Nation upon earth, that has more substantial reasons for feeling proud of its history, and splendid achievements than America has. As to whether it should exultingly manifest a spirit of pride before the whole world is altogether another question. Pride and shame, two opposing feelings or attributes of mind and heart, sensitive and powerful, when aroused, spring from principle and conduct. We are to dwell more specifically upon the subject of shame as it stands related to National life. And note at the outset that as the violation of the principles of truth, justice and honor subjects individuals to humiliation, degradation and shame; likewise Nations violating the same principles are subjected to shame.

We will turn at once to the consideration of the subject for discussion, namely: "Drunkenness, the shame of our Nation." There is no loftier, purer and nobler sentiment of patriotism than is expressed, in lifting hand and voice against intemperance. There is no sublimer conception of humane and philanthropic work and duty, than that which finds expression in the determined and unfailing efforts that are being made by men and women throughout this country to stay the tide of intemperance. It is, indeed, difficult to comprehend how any person endowed with these natural attributes of character, charity and humane sympathy, can calmly contemplate the wreck, ruin and desolation wrought by intemperance, upon either bank of the stream,—in America and in England; and throughout the world;—and not realize the reproach and shame intemperance casts upon those Nations that encourage, foster and protect the vicious and destructive liquor traffic.

It is by reason of the fact that strong drink, degrades and disgraces a people and a nation, that, men abound who are ready to wage an hostile opposition against the introduction and existence of this blighting curse. In this they are actuated by human motives; animated by lofty aims and purposes; and inspired by a sublime view of man's duty and obligations to his fellow man. There is a tinge of grandeur, of royalty, yea, of divinity, in man's recognizing and being influenced by the relations he sustains to his fellow man. No man can live this life to himself, if he rises to eminence and acquires wealth he will find men less fortunate looking up to him for counsel, for a word of influence, or for aid. Or if he should descend to the depths of degradation, he will find those who are willing to lend him a helping hand. This humane disposition, principle or characteristic of mankind finds expression in ten thousand ways; and does much to make life tolerable. That broad and noble charity that extends its helping hand, to those who need it, that seeks to alleviate suffering, to rescue and reclaim the fallen, has done much to save humanity from descending to those depths of degradation, from which it would have despaired to have risen again. It is this charity, this brotherly love, that binds mankind together. It circumvents the globe. And humanity everywhere feels that its magic spell or subtle influence unites the races, tribes and nations of earth in one common family and one brotherhood.

Words are not equal to the task in portraying the sublimity of the character of that disposition and zeal of men, to interest themselves in the welfare of their fellow man ; to struggle against the wrong, and to erect barriers in the way of the tide of abuse and lawlessness, and to alleviate the suffering and sorrow that follow in their wake. Such deeds are wreathed with the halo of divinity; such principles are savored with the divine ; such charity is God-like. If then it is an assertion of a true and noble manhood, if it is lofty and sublime, to lift up the fallen, to counteract, when it is possible, the blighting influence of intemperance ; then the shame that attaches to our Nation, in suffering intemperance to exist, stands out in boldness by way of contrast. For in this we have a contrast of the sublime with the infamous—the regal, exalted and noble with the lowly, the sordid and the vicious.

Somebody, somewhere, or in some way, merits the pitiless scorn, the criticism, and the righteous rebuke of every friend of humanity, of every one who has in the past and is now lifting hand and voice, or putting forth an effort calculated in some way to alleviate sorrow or to improve the condition of mankind, suffering and groaning beneath the burden of a thousand ills and inflictions. Intemperance exists. And its very existence makes the daily history of our Nation more hideous than a nightmare vision of barbarism. Somebody, somewhere or in some way, are responsible for this. There is no excuse for the existence of intemperance, in the vicious form in which it inflicts our Nation, and the man who offers an excuse for it is morally guilty for its existence ; at least to the extent that an individual man can be guilty for a National offense or crime. Our Nation, or our Statesmen, the Nation's Representatives furnish an excuse for intemperance and make its existence legal.

Surely if a degree of infamy and shame attaches to the liquor traffic, those who find and excuse for the existence of such a traffic, are morally, and, we might as well say, legally, responsible for it. Surely if our statesmen have it in their power to crush, by one legislative stroke, the great rum traffic of our Nation, and have not the disposition to exercise that power, then they are responsible for intemperance and its frightful consequences. And what shall we say of them when we reflect that they have legalized this damning traffic? If our Senators, our Congressmen and our Legislators, and our municipal authorities take it upon themselves to legalize the rum traffic, knowing that the most serious and distressing consequences result from it, ought they not, from a high sense of honor, to be willing to stand legally responsible for the consequences, whatever they may be, that result from such a source? But no one thinks of imputing the heart-rending crimes that result from drunkenness to the men in high places who legalized the sale of liqour, instead of banishing the accursed thing from out our land. Perhaps when they come to stand before the judgment of the great throne, and the Recording Angel opens the books and reads the history and legislative acts of their life when they lived on earth, and figured in the management and government of nations; perhaps then and there it may appear that the shame of drunkenness which our Nation has endured, may be justly imputed to them, and may throughout eternity rest as a burden upon their souls. But now, and here upon this stage of time where the lurid, hellish acts in this drama of drunkenness, crime and debauchery is being played, no one is responsible but the actor in the tragic play, and sometimes they want to excuse him because of his inebriety.

In no case, and by no one, is it considered proper to hold the statesmen who legalized drunkenness responsible for the vicious crimes and cruel murders committed in the name of strong drink. Not even the saloon-keeper, who fills the glass with the fateful poison and puts it to the lips of the man whose passions it fires and whose brain it maddens as a preparation for the commission of a cruel murder, is held responsible for the crime, or is regarded as an accessory to it. The murderer, fresh from the tragic scene of bloodshed and the dying groans of his victim, is hurried off to prison; at length he is summoned from the prison to the gallows; and while he is swinging from the end of the rope into eternity, his accessory, the man who furnished him with the lurid, flaming poison to drink, sits at ease in his guilded haunt of crime, puffing his cigar, or standing behind the bar industriously preparing another victim for the commission of some hellish deed. He is not regarded in the eyes of the law as an accessory to the crimes which he prepares and equips men to commit.

The statesman has legalized his business, and to convict him as an accessory to the crime of murder would be to involve the statesman too. Yet if it had not been for that glass of strong drink, the murder would not have been committed; and had not the statesman legalized the traffic, the saloon-keeper would not have sold him the glass of strong drink; and had the glass of strong drink not been dispensed by the saloon-keeper there would have been no murder committed. But what is still worse than anything we have said is this: Following near the poor victim, marching from the prison to the scaffold, guarded by the officers, fettered it may be in irons, we hear him muttering with trembling lips and sobbing breath, this charge that fastens the conviction of guilt upon his accessories: "Had it not been for that maddening drink I would not be going to meet such a terrible fate."

Dear friends of temperance, it will take eternity, at least it will take the judgment of the great Eternal Throne to disentangle this mighty complication and to place the guilt of the fearfully prevalent murders committed in the name of liquor where they belong. The man who commits murder under the influence of liquor says that he is not responsible for what he did when his brain was crazed with the fiery, maddening beverage of destruction. And I am inclined to think his point is well taken. I doubt not but that the man who furnished him the lurid drink is more guilty in the sight of God than the murderer himself. And would you be surprised if I should say that perhaps God regards those men whose votes legalized the vicious and criminal traffic of strong drink, as more guilty than all the rest. And if we go back to the Bible we find that it is not silent upon this point. Two thousand years ago, an inspired writer gave the world to understand that the guilt and woe of drunkenness rests upon the man who puts the glass to his neighbor's lips.

I dwell upon this point, for it is of importance. Murder is a solemn and terrible thing. Seven hundred of them are caused every year by intemperance in our country. And in so serious a matter it is of great importance to know who, if anybody, is responsible for it. But this is only one of the roaring, grinding floodgates of destruction which the rum traffic has opened for humanity. It is only one of the causes for shame and reproach to our Nation.

I do not relish quoting statistics. Besides, every one is, doubtless, more or less familiar with the figures that reveal the fearful ravages of strong drink. But we can profitably devote some time to the consideration of them. The statistics which I shall quote refer to drunkenness in the United States only.

Intemperance sends to prison every year one hundred thousand men and women.

Twenty thousand children are sent to the workhouse annually by strong drink.

Seven hundred murders are committed every year as the result of intemperance.

Three hundred thousand children are made orphans every year by this dreadful evil.

And seventy-five thousand lives are destroyed every year.

Three hundred thousand people die from the effects of intemperance either directly or indirectly. Some by murder instigated by drink, some by starvation, others by accidents caused by drunkenness.

There are 800,000 paupers in America caused by liquor.

282,000 persons are confined in prisons and penitentiaries because of liquor.

Let us estimate the amount of liquor used in our country annually.

There are seventy-five million gallons of spirituous liquors used every year in the United States; or to put it in other words, the manufacture of that liquor consumes twenty-seven million bushels of grain, which would have made one billion and eighty million pounds of flour; the barrels required to hold which would reach from Philadelphia to Omaha.

Besides this there are five hundred million gallons of beer consumed in the United States annually.

Let us look for a moment at the expense to which the liquor traffic subjects our people and our Nation.

Virginia drinks up her entire wheat crop annually. The liquor drink in Louisiana costs forty-seven million dollars, annually, or more than the combined cotton, sugar and rice crop amounts to.

New York City spends sixty million dollars annually for wines and liquors.

And offsets this by spending the pitiful sum of four millions annually for educational purposes.

Three hundred and seventy-five million dollars are spent annually for beer alone. Seven dollars and fifty cents for every men, woman and child.

This expense alone is one-fourth more than the expense of running the United States Government.

In round numbers the liquor traffic costs the people of the United States one billion of dollars cash, annually.

There are half a million of people in the country who cannot read; they could have been educated for one-twentieth part of the amount spent for strong drink.

The cost of liquor in two years time would amount to enough to build seven lines of railroads across the continent, each 3,000 miles long at $20,000 per mile, put on two million dollars worth of rolling stock; build another railroad around the world, and put on one million dollars worth of rolling stock; and then have five hundred million dollars left with which to educate the poor and build Ellemosynary institutions.

The liquor traffic costs every inhabitant of the United States $40 tax per year. Eighty per cent. of all the government tax going to pay the expenses of the infamous and infernal liquor traffic.

One dollar out of every ten of the hard-earned wages of the working man is devoured in some way by the rum devil which haunts the land. Of course, I have gleaned these statistics from various sources, and will add one more statement of peculiar interest:

"THE DRINK SHOP'S RECORD.—When the war closed seventeen years ago and the Nation had its dead sons and widowed wives, sad mothers and children, it had an enormous debt. It had cost the United States Government, the States, and cities, and towns of the North no less than $6,165,237,000 to to complete the war. It had cost the South not less than $2,000,000,000, making a total expense to the country of $8,165,237,000.

It is a sad and terrible record. But let it be remembered that every year since the war closed the people of our country have paid alone for alcoholic drinks more than $600,000,000. Or in fifteen years the sum of $9,000,000,-000. In this we count, not the vast and far-reaching and enormous sums of money expended and lost through degradation and crime, which the poor and the rich have expended through accursed drink, but simply the drink bill of the Nation.

The reader may add to this the cost of crime, poverty, idiocy, loss of productive labor, etc. But the drink bill alone of these fifteen years would have paid every dollar of the cost of the war, and left remaining on hand for good uses $834,783,000. This is a commonly known fact. It is enough to startle our Nation, and make the Christian people reel with wonder. What have we for these wasted resources of our fair land? What remuneration comes to us for the expenditure of money for the seething, liquid fire? Ask our homes of disgrace, poverty, and ignorance! Ask our homes of sorrow, of shame, of bereavement, of broken vows, and utter helplessness! Ask our city prisons, our jails, our penitentiaries, and our insane asylums; all filled with victims of strong drink! Ask the court-room, the poor fellow pinioned on the gallows and dropping into eternity; ask these what we have to show for our drink bill!

During four years of civil war it was estimated that 1,000,000 lives were lost, but in these seventeen years which have passed since they fell, this war of intemperance has murdered not less than seven or eight times that number of our fellow beings. Natis, the king of Sparta, had erected a sorcerous figure of his wife Apego, royally clad, and into the hideous embrace of this gorgeously-clad machine, he thrust those he would punish. The sharp irons which were concealed under the clothing of the hellish machine proved the death of many a poor man who was clasped in its iron arms. Such is the awful, and inhuman, and hellish structure, the whisky traffic, whose sorcerous and lecherous arms are around the Nation."

There are costs and burdens imposed upon our people, by the traffic of strong drink, that cannot be estimated or comprised in figures. We may number or limit the aggregate of the lives it costs in one way and another, but we cannot estimate the tears, the groans of anguish and the broken hearts it has cost. Neither can we estimate the possibilities for the accomplishments of good it has thwarted, and the promising lives it has blasted. There is no basis of calculation by which we can arrive at an estimate of the suffering, sorrow, distress, heart rending, and blighted hopes intemperance costs our people and our Nation. Its frightful ravages have no parallell. The desolation and devastating terrors of plagues, pestilences, famines, and war—the work of all these aggregated—does not equal the wreck and ruin of this devastating, far reaching and wide encircling curse of intemperance.

The skeletons of its victims piled up in a massive heap would reach the skies. The tears it has shed would flood the earth as the waters cover the sea, and the blood it has shed would dye that flood to the deepest crimson. My dear friends, reflect if you will upon the accumulated woe, misery, suffering and death following in the wake of this horrible, monstrous evil of the nineteenth century, and then think upon the shame and reproach it casts upon our Nation. Still, beyond what we had already said about the sin and desolation wrought by drunkenness, it is unspeakably sad to reflect that men of the brightest intellect are swept down in this vortex of ruin. That the noblest specimens of manhood are crushed by its power. That position, wealth and grandeur vanish before its lurid, flaming, hissing breath. Those who have once stood high, fall to the lowest depths of degradation and shame, when they once become the victims of strong drink.

"A STORY OF A WRECKED LIFE.—The most thrilling and sadly suggestive temperance lecture is the sight of a once noble, talented man left in ruins by intoxicating drink. A Washington letter tells of a ragged beggar, well known in the streets of that city, who once held an important command in the army, having been promoted, for personal bravery, from a cavalry lieutenant to nearly the highest rank in military service. One night recently, when he had been too successful in begging liquor to sate his craving, and while lying helplessly drunk in the rear part of a Third Street saloon, some men thought to play a joke on him by stealing his shirt, and proceeded to strip him.

"Underneath his shirt, and suspended by a string from his neck, was a small canvass bag, which the men opened, and found it contained his commission as Brevet Major-General, two congratulatory letters—one from Gen. Grant and one from President Lincoln—a photograph of a little girl, and a curl of hair—a "chestnut shadow" that doubtless one day crept over the brow of some loved one.

"When these things were discovered, even the half-drunken men who found them felt a respect for the man's former greatness, and pity for his fallen condition, and quietly returned the bag and its contents to where they found them, and replaced the sleeper's clothes upon him.

"When a reporter tried to interview the man, and endeavored to learn something of his life for the past few years, he refused to communicate anything.

"He cried like a child when told how his right name and position were ascertained, and, with tears trickling down his cheeks, said:—

"'For God's sake, sir, don't publish my degradation, or my name at least, if you are determined to say something about it. It is enough that I know myself how low I have become. Will you please promise that much? It will do no good, but will do my friends a great deal of harm, as, fortunately, they think I died in South America, where I went at the close of the war.'

"Intemperance and the gambling table, he said, had wrought his ruin."

And then again, if we could in some way aggregate or estimate the crimes of ten thousand different degrees and classes, caused by liquor, we would be appalled by the enormity and character of them. The Judges of our courts in every part of the country are well-nigh unanimous in declaring the opinion that nine-tenths of the crimes that come before the criminal courts of our country are directly attributable to strong drink. Crime of every class and order finds its chief abetter in the drinking saloon. They are the moral pest-houses of the land. And within or beneath the shadow of the eaves of those haunts there is blight, suffering, disease and death. The drinking-saloon is literally the gateway of Hell to any man who enters it. It is the guilded haunt of immorality, vice and crime, the lair of Satan, the murderer of the soul. Alas! what may we not truthfully say about intemperance! It is as an omnipotent Angel of destruction, brooding with dark, shadowy wings over the whole world, and beneath the shadow of those wings the happiness and hopes of millions of people are perishing to-day.

But the object of a temperance lecture should be, not so much to portray the ruin and desolation wrought by intemperance, as to speak a few earnest word of encouragement to those who are at work resisting the tide of this mighty current of evil. And while the contemplation of the results of intemperance is enough to thrill those with enthusiasm who are waging an opposition to it, it is, nevertheless, well enough not to become enthusiasts in this work; for the results of this work must be accomplished by degrees. From a humanitarian standpoint and motive, we desire the speedy downfall of this Satanic sway of power; but we cannot accomplish what we desire upon the impulse of the moment. If we besiege and crush the throne of King Alcohol, and take the mighty citadel of intemperance after years of campaign of skilled generalship, diplomacy and hard fighting, we may feel both proud and grateful over the victory.

We would like to destroy intemperance at once, with one mignty stroke, and then be permitted to live for awhile and enjoy the fruitions, blessings and quiet of life in a land freed from the devastating, pestilential scourge of strong drink. But not so—life with man is a battle; and destroying intemperance is a warfare. The time may come when intemperance will go down in the clash of battle, the campaign ended, the soldiers ground their arms and return home to live in peace and enjoy the fruitions, the victory secured for them. But it is scarcely advisable for us to indulge in the hope of sharing this blissful participation. But if we are intelligently waging an opposition to intemperance, then we must associate God and Heaven with our work. And what we do must be done in His name and for His sake, and not simply for ourselves and for humanity. And, friends of temperance, it is a poorly fought battle that is not fought in the name of God—"the God of Hosts." That most fascinating of all the world's histories, the Old Testament Scriptures, tell us that God, Jehovah, the "God of hosts," took part in the battles in the olden times, that His influence was felt in them; that He planned the battles for His people; that He directed and guided them, that the generals and leaders of His people were godly men. And nowhere do we find that the people of God ever lost a battle, in those mighty warfares far back in ancient times. So to-day, dear friends in the great moral warfare against evil, against crime, against intemperance, against the world, God, the God of Hosts, is on our side; we feel His influence; He is planning our battles; and, after awhile, we will win an illustrious and final victory in His name; for He will not suffer his people to be defeated. The warfare over intemperance is a well defined war between God and His hosts, and the Devil and his hosts, and what poor, trembling soul among us doubts but that God and His hosts will win the triumph.

Our war against intemperance is of no purpose, if God—the God of Heaven of humanity and of love, is not our General. And if we do not associate Heaven with the reformation of the drunkard, the drunkard is not with reforming. For if the drunkard after he is reformed from intemperance is to go on down to perdition, he had as well have died a drunkard as any other way.

God is honored by the work we are doing in the cause of temperance. He is honored by our efforts, whether those efforts avail anything or not. He is honored all the same whether we win the victory, or whether we do not win it. In His own good time He will give us the victory. We honor Him by showing our fidelity to Him and our faith in Him by fighting on whether we win the victory or not. In this we exhibit that faith that most pleases Him.

When President Garfield *was laid low upon the couch of pain and suffering, our Nation, yea, the whole Christian world, knelt at his side, and prayed God to spare his life. But God in His wise providence did not choose to do this. But God was honored by those faithful prayers. And the people done just what they should have done. For prayer is not so much—praying with the expectation of getting what we have asked for; as it trusting God, whether we get what we ask for or not. This is the true spirit of prayer; not exacting what we pray for, but trusting God without a thought of what the answer shall be. It was a grand triumph for God when this whole Christian Nation—and in fact the whole Christian world knelt at the bedside of our suffering President and in simple faith and dependence implored God to spare his life. This humility, this trustfulness and recognition of God honored Him. It was this that pleased God. He was under no obligations to answer that prayer, by granting the people what they asked for. But the people showed the right spirit in trusting Him, regardless of whether He granted their reuqests or denied them.

written in 1882.

It seems to me that that was the grandest victory God ever won over Satan. It was certainly the grandest exhibition of loyal faith and trust that the Christian people ever manifested toward God.

So in this cause of temperance, we must work on, toil on and fight on, trusting God for the results. These are parallell cases. How would it have done for our people to have gathered around the President's bedside, in silence and no one among us in all the land, lifted up the voice of supplication and prayer to God to spare his life. An Infidel Nation might have done that. But a Christian Nation like ours could never have been guilty of such a thing. And in the cause of temperance, the cause may look hopeless to some, but how would it do for us to fold our hands and stand by in silence, conscious that the demon of rum and strong drink, is destroying the vitality and life of our Nation, and not lift hand or voice in defiance to the work of this monstrous evil and blighting curse. Had we not better enlist in a campaign against intemperance, trusting that we will win the victory, even though we should be defeated. If we do not do this, we are unworthy of the name of a Christian people and a Christian Nation.

Finally, dear friends, we are trusting to two sources in being able to cope with and overcome, our adversary,—intemperance; one is a Christian public sentiment, and the other is Legislation. It is probable that they will be very intimately associated, when the crises comes when the liquor traffic shall be crushed to the earth. I have faith in Legislation to cope with this giant evil. But Legislation is feeble and helpless without a Christian public sentiment to back and sustain it. In the first place we cannot get Legislation against the liquor trade until we have developed and fostered a moral public sentiment against the traffic. And it is clearly evident that a great work remains to be done. A Legislative act may be speedily accomplished, properly signed and proclaimed a law, and that law enforced. But before we can secure Legislation against the manufacture and sale of liquor, we have got to bring this matter in all its hideous proportions before the people and before the Legislatures of our country.

Eventually this will be accomplished. And I do not think the day is a great way off. Soon I believe we shall hear the shout of victory, and the Hosannas of praise to God for His deliverance. We have ten fold better reasons for encouragement, than we have for discouragement. For those who are for us are greater than those who are against us. What the temperance people want is more faith, more earnestness and concentrated action. We need earnest workers and earnest speakers in the cause of temperance. There is earnestness on the other side. Let us make the spirit of our temperance guild more strict that its influence may be greater. And let us not be ashamed that we are working, talking and praying for the success of the temperance cause. But let the shame rest upon those who are abetting intemperance; let it rest upon our Nation. But let us do our duty faithfully and manfully, and God will own and eventually crown our efforts with illustrious victory. Such a triumph of the temperance cause is of vital interest to humanity; for not until Legal Prohibition shall have been accomplished, will liberty—in our fair land —be Crowned with justice, the pillars of our National temple made secure, humanity sheltered from blight and sorrow, and the cause of Christ materially advanced in the earth. It is not a mere illusion of hope to expect the consumation of this sublime purpose and end. Already the prospects are brightening, and faith in the ultimate triumph of temperance as well as the cause of justice and truth is strengthening. The evening shadows of the nineteenth century is subdued, and mellow rays are falling upon the pathway of this generation; and we are watching—with mingled gloom and hope, mingled disappointment and expectancy—the golden light of its sinking sun. Soon the dawn of another century will awaken the world. May the rays of its sun be pure. May its breath be as that of the eternal morning. May its light in bright effulgence break upon the world as the herald of a better day, as the harbinger of peace and triumph to a race so long wearied and burdened with oppression and wrong.

Prohibition Founded in Reason and Philosophy.

Is prohibition founded in reason and philosophy, is the complex and difficult subject for consideration in this lecture? The temperance question, within the last three or four years, both in this country and in Europe, has sprung to the surface, agitating the minds of men and society generally, like some monstrous animal of the deep, lashing the waves into commotion. But this figure is a feeble illustration. The agitation of the minds of the people to-day can better be likened to a great earthquake in the ocean, which rocks that body of water until every drop in the great illimitable basin has been moved and disturbed, setting in motion waves that go plunging in fury across the bosom of the mighty waters, raising the tides until in their fury they leap their bounds, and sweep the shores of a continent.

But some one says, the picture is overdrawn. Well perhaps it is. But the temperance controversy is increasing in scope and interest; and it is only a question of a little while, when every man, woman and child upon this continent and in this great world in which we live will be disturbed and moved by the great irrepressable temperance question. It is a vital living issue, and goes straight as an arrow to the heart the conscience and intellect of men. It is a question that springs up in the pathway of Christian civilization, and challenges the respect and consideration of every patriot, every philanthropist and every Christian man in the world. This theme of temperance which has been kindled upon the altar of every Christian heart has become a consuming and an unquenchable flame, and like "Alladen's Lamp," it will burn day and night forever, and the whole world shall see its light and feel its melting heat.

The temperance question which is agitating the minds of the people springs from Christian motives and human eimpulses. Men standing in the Theatre of life, look about them and see the degradation and ruin caused by strong drink, survey the devastation and terror of drunkenness, and calmly decide in their own heart and convictions that such wreck and ruin is not only unchristian, but that it is inhuman ; and that, if possible, a traffic that leads either directly or indirectly to such results ought to be forbidden by the sanctions of society and prohibited by law. Men of such convictions and principles band themselves together and we call that a temperance society. And the principles they advocate comprise the temperance question. The men who comprise temperance societies are composed of two classes—men who have Christian hearts, and men who have humane hearts; men who champion and engage heart and hand in the temperance work because they love God; and men who engage in the work because they love humanity. But both classes are working hand-in-hand in the great work of temperance reform. The best elements of society, the most intellectual men of the world, the Ministry, the Press, the Christian Statesman, have championed the temperance cause and principles. The great temperance army thus formed, and which is so great that it cannot be numbered is gaining ground and is moving forward, facing its opposition unaffrighted and undismayed, nerved for the conflict as soldiers are nerved when fighting for home and native land.

The great opposition or opposing host of which we speak, is the liquor traffic and the element of society that champion the liquor interest customs, etc. The line of battle between these two armies have been fairly drawn. These armies have come together and are facing each other upon the field of battle, ready apparently for the conflict that is to settle this great issue. But just before the first gun is fired, a flag of truce comes from the enemy asking that hostilities be delayed until the question can be discussed and decided whether it is founded in reason or phylosophy, that the liquor traffic should be suppressed by force. Consequently the question must be opened again and discussed in all its bearings, that it may be more conscientiously and fully understood. For it cannot be that men who profess to be actuated by Christian and humane motives will engage in the accomplishment of a work that is at once irrational and unjust. It is for these reasons briefly stated that we must continue to agitate and discuss this temperance question. The truth in its relation to this great problem must be made manifest. It must shine forth with the lustre, with which the jewelled stars in the heavens shine down upon our pathway. It must shine until every mind and heart is radiated with its splendor.

Liquor dealers and men who indulge in ardent spirits, raise the cry that we must not press this question of prohibition, as it invades the realm of personal rights and personal liberty; that such a measure is not only unjust but that it is not founded in reason or philosophy. Temperance men have decided these and kindred questions to the satisfaction of their own minds. But they have not quite succeeded in convincing one-half or the majority of the people of this country that their views are correct throughout. Hence the necessity of a little more discussion upon these points. These questions have been discussed a thousand times. But the discussion must not cease until this temperance issue has been finally decided.

This specifiic question before us—is prohibition founded in reason or philosophy—it seems to me comprises well nigh every other temperance question, and practically covers the whole ground of temperance discussion. It is about equivalent to asking, "is it right, just and honorable, and have you the moral right to invade the sanctity of a mans social and domestic customs," and say to him, "you shall or shall not drink what you please, you shall or shall not drink ales, wines, rum, brandy or whisky?" Those things are destructive to life, and because of the personal interest I feel in your wellfare and happiness, I take it upon myself to interfere with your free moral agency in this matter and prevent you from drinking strong drink to your destruction. And if it is decided

that you have the moral right to thus interfere with a man's social and domestic customs of life—then the question comes up to be answered, "have you
the right to forcibly prohibit drinking by invoking the majesty of the law, and
by calling to your aid the Legislation of this State and of this Nation in accomplishing this end.   Of course it is admitted that you have the right to persuade
a drunkard—if you can—to give up his bestial habit of drink and to reform
and be a sober man again.   But when it comes to forcibly interfering with a
mans drinking rum, gin and whisky, even to his distruction—that is altogether
a different question.

As has been said, temperance people have already decided this question
in their own minds.   But the question has often been discussed flippantly and
with injustice to the opposing element,   As for myself personally, I confess
that this is one of the most serious problems that ever in my life has come up
for consideration.   And I believe that, next to moral responsibility to God,
this is the most serious qaestion with which the world has to deal to-day.   Yet
it seems to me that it should not take a man long to decide in his mind as to
the right or wrong of interfering with another man's personal liberty or invading
his domestic rights, when by so doing he is saving that man's life.   Is it un-
reasonable and unjust, and is it morally wrong to interfere with a man's course
of conduct, when that man's life is involved or jeopardized by his course of
conduct.   Can it be that I have not the moral right, the legal right, and the
rational right to forcibly interfere with a man's deliberately taking his own life,
and that, too, regardless of what means he is employing for the accomplishment
of that purpose?   Can it be that any measure is unjust, and an invasion of
personal liberty, when the design and purpose of that measure is the protection
of human life from death?

The term personal liberty has become a misnomer, as it were, at least it has
become misleading.   The opposition to temperance reform have sought of late
to give this phrase, personal liberty, a peculiarly important and sacred meaning
when using it in the discussion of the temperance question.   The phrase,
"personal liberty," has been set up as a barrier against the advance movement
of temperance workers.   The opposition has said: Here is a line drawn; take
off your shoes, for the ground whereon you stand is sacred.   You may approach
to this line, but you must not cross over, for if you cross this line which we
have drawn, you invade the sanctity of personal liberty, and that is a crime
against God and man.   Now, that is all very well as an argument, but really
what foundation has such an argument?   And besides, are not the rum drinkers and rum sellers a nice lot of people to talk about the sacredness and
sanctity of personal liberty?   Erect a monument of granite before their eyes,
and inscribe upon it the statistic of intemperance, the work of their hand, the
destruction and ruin of prosperous business enterprises, the wrecked homes, the
blasted lives, the crime, poverty, insanity, suffering and wretchedness springing
from intemperance, and ask them if such fruit is the legitimate result of
personal liberty.

But suppose or admit that prohibition is an invasion of personal liberty;
and there can be no question but that it is—for argue this question as you may
interfering with what a man desires to eat or drink is interfering with his per-

sonal and God given liberty—but even so admitting this to be true, is not such an interference warranted? Is there not something in this world more sacred than personal liberty? The champions of the liquor traffic have not made a mistake in raising this point about prohibition being an invasion of personal liberty, their mistake has been in overestimating the sacredness and importance of personal liberty. Saloon men say personal liberty is sacred and must be protected. But what does the saloon man mean by personal liberty? He simply means that he individually must have the unmolested right to debauch this Nation, wreck its homes, and send its inhabitants reeling down to a drunkard hell. He means that he must have the inviolate right to sell rum, and that the Nation must take the consequences and bear the burdens. He means that his own individual right to earn a livelihood by selling rum is more sacred to him than the lives, the homes, the happiness and prosperity of this great Nation.

Admit that prohibition is an invasion of personal liberty, what is the object of this invasion? It is manifestly to save the lives of men, to save the homes of our nation, to save everything that is sacred, to save everything in our country of a perishable character that is worth saving; for if the devastating work of selling rum is continued in our country for the next fifty years, as it has been carried on for the past two decades, there will be nothing left us of a sacred character. Then looking the rum dealer straight in the face, and admitting that prohibition is an invasion of personal liberty, and that too after giving this term personal liberty, its more sacred meaning, we ask the straightforward question, is not this invasion warranted and justified? The only object that temperance men have for pressing this measure of prohibition to the front is, that the rum traffic is debauching the nation, ruining homes, destroying lives, blighting happiness, hindering prosperity and retarding the progress of christian civilization.

But the rum seller steps to the front and says, the measure is an invasion of personal liberty. Very well then, if that is an invasion of what you choose to call personal liberty, then we will have to invade. For such a barrier as this which they have set up is but a feeble resistance to the designs and purposes of temperance men, to save the lives of men, to rescue the Nation itself from debauchery and all the devastating terrors of the accursed rum traffic. Liquor men say, "personal liberty" is sacred; but if they mean by this phrase the unrestricted right and privilege to sell and to drink rum to their fill, entailing immeasurable suffering and sorrow upon humanity, then they must be taught the lesson that there is something more sacred in this world than personal liberty. A political measure is not in any very broad or true sense an invasion of personal liberty, when it is calculated and designed for the patriotic and humane purpose of saving lives, protecting homes and promoting national prosperity and happiness.

If a great evil threatens our nation's existence we need not be particular about what means we shall employ for the purpose of staying the tide or turning the channel of destruction. So in dealing with this curse of rum, we need not be over nice or fastiduous as to what means we shall employ for the purpose of staying this tide of ruin and of death. If a man is over-board and floundering in the waves would you call it an invasion of personal liberty to rescue him? Now in conscience and in reason, does it make any difference as to how a man is perishing as to whether you shall rescue him, or as to what means you shall employ in rescueing him? Press this one argument alone, that the rum traffic is destructive of human life; that in round numbers throughout the world one million of men and women lose their lives in some way connected or associated with the rum traffic, and you have an argument favoring prohibition against which no man can lift his voice or raise his hand. You have an argument in this at once so formidable and terrifying that it ought to hush to a mute silence forever every voice that to-day champion the hellish liquor traffic. And yet the liquor men cry out, be careful in pressing your prohibition measures that you do not invade the sanctity of personal liberty and individual rights. Oh! what a travesty of truth and reason! What a mockery! What a burlesque in argument! That "Old Dragon," which is the Devil and Satan, with all his cunning and wiles never coined a more subtle lie and put it on the tongue of a man than this argument about prohibition being an infringement upon or an invasion of personal, liberty! It is a deceptive argument and a lie worthy of his Satanic Majesty.

The righteous design and purpose of Legislative prohibition measures is to liberate men from the thralldom and curse of strong drink. To strike from their hands and their feet the shackles of intemperance. But men say I recoil from the thought of temperance by law. But this universe is subject to law, and this world is run by law, and the people that dwell in it are governed by law. Verily, God, the great lawgiver of the universe has subjected Himself to law; it emanated from His throne and flashed to the circling bounds of the universe. The Bible is a very good temperance text book. It was Paul who taught in the Bible the blessed doctrine of total abstinence for another's sake. It does not, however forbid or attempt to prohibit a man from drinking strong drink if he wants too. It simply tells him that if he does he will be damned. The Bible in many things may be very properly classed with the statutes of our Nation, and as a standard authority in the matter of civil jurisprudence. But in the matter of intemperance it lays down a principal by which the people are to be governed, instead of seeking to enforce prohibition as a civil law.

Christ came eating and drinking and they called him a winebibber and a glutton. Had he not have come in this way they might have said even worse things of Him. Evil disposed, and we may say, silly minded men of to-day, in pleading their rights to indulge in moderate drinking often cite the miracles of Christ turning water into wine. But this is a delusion. It is false reasoning. It is sheer cavil to say that the wine which Christ made and used at the wedding feast at the marriage in Canaa, was such deleterious, inflaming, diluted and adulterated stuff as is bottled up, or sold to customers over the bar of the rum saloon of to-day. Much might be said upon this subject, but I do not propose to discuss it in its length and breadth at this time. It is enough, to say that it is inconsistent and irrational to confound the wine which Christ made from water, with the intoxicating and adulterated wines used to-day. I am aware that it was said that the wine was of the best quality, and that they had to put it in the new bottles as the old bottles were not strong enough to hold it, but even so I do not think that there is any evidence to show that the wine He made was inflaming and intoxicating.

Again, Christ's public ministry occurred at a period when there was but little if any drunkenness in the world; when intemperance was not a National curse, as it is to-day. Therefore it was not necessary for even this Divine Teacher to be so guarded in his utterances, as it would have been had he lived in this age. I apprehend that if Christ lived in this age, when drunkenness is rampant, and wine-drinking is the scourge of the earth, that he would not encourage wine-drinking even in the mild way he did; but rather that he would advise that all the wine in the land be poured into the river and carried down to the sea.

Men who have been in the habit of drinking moderately, pursuing the custom probably through their lives, yet who never knew the power and effect of drink as an intoxicating stimulant naturally feel that it is well-nigh an intolerable invasion of their personal liberty and rights to enact a law putting all kinds of spirituous liquors out of their reach. Now this is plausible reasoning and an argument that demands our consideration and respect, but we cannot admit that it is valid or essentially just, for if we do, all argument favoring prohibition goes to pieces at once. Some one says: "What are you going to do with this seemingly just claim? Are you going to trample the rights of the people beneath your feet?" Yes, I reply, we are going to do this, if that is the language you choose to use in describing our course and action.— The temperance people of this country, if they can get votes enough,—and I think it will only be a short time when we will have a surplus,—are going to banish thus accursed thing of strong drink from out of the Nation, so that even those who do not want to drink cannot get to where it is.

Now I will tell you why they are going to do this, and why they have their hearts set upon this achievment. It is not because the temperance people want to interfere with the God-given right and liberty of any man. But it is like this: You put strong drink—as we are doing now—within the reach of every man, and about one out of every ten will drink himself to death. If he does no do this, he will get drunk, and in his debauch and frenzy will kill his neighbor or friend, or his wife or child. If you leave strong drink within the reach of every man as it is now, so many murders, so many suicides, so many deaths, so much crime, poverty, suffering and sorrow will spring from its use that it will harrow the hearts of our people, mar the symmetry and grandeur of our Christian civilization, and destroy the pride of National existence. It has well-nigh done this now. And it is this turbulent tide of ruin, of wretchedness and of woe following in the wake of drunkenness that has moved the hearts of men to undertake this great temperance reform. And when this great reform is accomplished the moderate toper and the casual drinker will have to fare the same as the besotted inebriate in the matter of deprivation of drink. In the fulness of time the accursed draught will be wrested from the hands of every one. The moderate drinker will perhaps have a more just reason to complain than the confirmed drunkard, but the stern arbitrament of the ballot will show no partiality, and show no respect of persons. The men who can give up drink and won't do it, will have to share with the helpless drunkard the extreme humiliation of being forcibly deprived of the privilege of the debasing indulgence.

Somebody preached a temperance sermon in a dozen words; they said: "If the custom of drinking only costs you a little to give it up, then give it up for your neighbors sake. If it costs you a great deal, then give it up for your own sake." But men have not got much magnanimity along this line. Oh ! that all men had the magnanimity of that Sainted Apostle Paul, who was willing to do anything for the sake of his brother. He was willing to abstain from drinking wine or from eating meat, or from anything that would cause his brother to stumble. But when we come to reflect upon this,—it wasn't magnanimity so much in Paul as it was the grace of God. Would that all men were christians, then we wouldn't need prohibitory laws. If men had the love of Christ in their hearts it wouldn't take long to settle this temperance question ; for this temperance question and all it implies is germain to Jesus Christ and the religion of divine revelation, and it is germain to every thing on this side of heaven that is true and good and holy.

We talk about temperance societies and prohibition parties accomplishing prohibitory Legislation; that is all well enough, but they are only helping on with the work. Temperance societies are the dashing waves upon the surface. The religion of Christ among our people is the mighty undercurrent and undertone of the sea in this great work of temperance reform. The church is essentially a temperance organization, not specifically, but in a general sense. It is the precurser in all temperance movements. The church is fairly the power behind the throne in the great work of moral temperance reform.

But again we revert briefly to the thought that prohibatory measures inflicts injustice and wrong upon the moderate or casual drinker. The man who takes an occasional glass says, "I am not harmed by the indulgence, neither is anyone else, therefore there is not one single reason why I should be forcibly deprived of this coveted pleasure and privilege." I dwell upon this point because this is, or will become, the shiboleth of the liquor party and advocates, but the argument is an hallucination, and is not founded in truth or in fact: and the theory in the light of reason instantly vanishes from sight. No man can touch the vile stuff we call whisky without being injured and debased morally and physically. It is a poison that blights and withers the intellect, corrupts the morals and taints the system of the man who drinks it however mildly. No man can drink a single glass of liquor and not feel its harmful effects, and the theory that a man can drink whisky moderately with impunity falls to the ground. It is a vicious falsehood, besides moderate drinkers eventually becomes drunkards; not all of them perhaps, but a large proportion of them do. The moderate drinker who opposes the abolition of the rum traffic, practically tabulates the statistics of the murders, death, crime, wretchedness and woe that springs from this source, and holding them before his face says, "I can tolerate and endure all this for the sake of having a rum hole convenient to me where I can have the delectable pleasure of taking an occasional glass and gratify my burning thirst with the fiery beverage. He practically says "no amount of wretchedness, poverty and woe entailed upon our country by strong drink can be so great and terrible as to induce me to forego the pleasure of occasional or moderate drinking.

Is this not so? Is this not true to the letter? We cannot have moderate drinking without having drunkenness, and all the dark category of crimes that follow it. But the moderate drinker calmly surveys the devastation and ruin that follows in the wake of drunkenness, and says: "Not even all this is formidable enough to induce me to abandon the custom of social drinking, or assent to the abolition of the liquor traffic." And if it is hinted that it will be abolished anyway, he complains that his rights and liberty are in peril. The moderate drinker loathes the drunkard. He says the man who cannot drink without getting drunk, or without making a fool of himself—as is his choice of language—ought not to touch it all. But he is forgetful of the fact that by the time the new beginner tests the experiment whether he can drink moderately without becoming a drunkard, he has contracted an appetite and thirst for strong drink which is uncontrollable. His power of will in the matter of abstaining from drink has passed beyond his control, and he is a helpless, hopeless drunkard. He is the man, infinitely more than the moderate drinker, who cannot abandon the fatal cup.

Abolish the liquor traffic and you either consciously or unconsciously of what you are doing banish with it nine-tenths of all the crimes which paint the daily history of this great Nation crimson. You ask for a proof of this. I refer you to the police and court records of New York City, of this city, or of any great city in the country. I point you to the published statistics that in this great Commonwealth of Kentucky, where whisky flows as freely as the water flows in the Ohio river, that there were 160 murders committed last year, while in the State of Maine, where the sale of whisky is prohibited, there were but one murder committed. We refer you to a recent statement of a Texas paper, that that State will average two killings a day. Drive the liquor trade out of the State and you will diminish the killing nine-tenths. If the statistics could be carefully gathered together, it would show at least one thousand murders resulting from strong drink annually in this country. It is a fair question then to ask, is it founded in reason or philosophy to prevent murder? If so, then is it not founded in reason or philosophy to prevent the sale of whisky, which more than any other case inflames the passions and leads to the commission of murder.

We use every precaution and protection to save men's lives. We legislate against murder, and punish criminal carelessness by which human life is jeopardized or destroyed. We do this not because men are so scarce that we cannot afford to loose one now and then—for men are plenty,—but we do this because human life is sacred. Then we ask in the name of humanity and in the name of justice. Have we not the right to legislate against the liquor traffic which ten times over more than all other causes combined leads to the commission of murder.

As we progress along in the work looking to legislative prohibition, the challenge comes, "is the principles of prohibition right." This challenge is not a simple construction of words, or an idle speculation ; neither is it intended to be so much driftwood thrown across the current of moral reform. The challenge comes from a legitimate source and demands respectful attention. If it did not originate it nevertheless finds logment in the mind and heart of intelligent, thoughtful and conscientious men; and Statesmen are muddling their brain with this mooted problem of legal enactment against the manufacture and sale of whisky. And when United States Senators, men famed for their intelligence and power of intellect, render a negative decision upon the advisability and justice of legal prohibition, it gives dignity and weight to the opposition, strengthens the hands of the whisky sellers, and suggests to the friends of temperance a more careful and conscientious review of the whole question; a question that involves so much cannot be too carefully considered, however this question of prohibition has been turned over and over and has been revolving around in mens minds for centuries upon centuries. And even to-day in this advanced age of enlightened christian sentiment, some of the Statesmen of America challenge the justice of prohibatory measures. Senator Bayard, and there is no Statesman in the Democratic party who ranks higher for judicious and conservative views upon questions of national importance, recently ventured the following expression of opinion. He says: "the spasms of prohibition action which are observable all over the country cannot last, for they are not founded, in reason or philosophy, and will only lead in a few years to the enactment of laws that are so inquisatorial and invasive of personal freedom and liberty, of conscience and action, that they will·be found impossible of execution, and if enacted will speedily be repealed.

This wonderful effusion of thought must have drained the great Senators mind. It is however, a clear and forcible condensation and expression of opinion, and when we reflect for a moment upon the position and eminence of the man who uttered this sentiment, they seem well calculated to make the friends of temperance tremble for the safety and the fate of their cherished temperance measures and principles; but when we reflect again, we remember that Senator Bayard was one of the men who stood up in the Halls of Congress twenty years ago and defended human slavery as a National institution. Slavery afterwards went down before the mighty clash of arms, and that too regardless of the opinion of Statesmen who sought to make the sacred constitution of this Government defend it. So when Mr. Bayard again ventures an opinion—and his opinion this time is upon the unconstitutionality and inconsistency of legal prohibition—there is a lurking thought in a great many persons mind that the Senator has again made a slight mistake, and that after all, prohibition may yet be accomplished.

Certainly the opinion of a United States Senator—especially one so eminent and so grandly and nobly endowed with humane impulses and rare culture as is Senator Bayard carries dignity and force, and is deserving of the most respectful consideration. But even so there is always a possibility of even a great man making a mistake. And certainly Mr. Bayard has made a mistake ; and I only speak of Senator Bayard as a prominent man on the side of the opposition, uttering an important declaration of opinion upon this grand national issue which is practically open and before the whole enlightened world to discuss and dispose of. Mr. Bayard practically says prohibition is out of the question ; it cannot be accomplished ; as a political measure, it is not founded in reason or philosophy. But it seems to me that this declaration of opinion is neither discreet nor warranted. He makes these declarations directly in the face of the fact that prohibition as a political measure is in practical and successful operation in nearly one-half the Union to-day. The States have, by the voice and suffrage of their people boldly declared in favor of local option, and local option—which is but local prohibition—is in practical operation in sections of every State in the Union. And in some States the counties in which local option is in successful operation and has been for a decade of years can be numbered by the scores.

But now the closing thought—how is legal prohibition to be accomplished? By the suffrage of the people—for moral suasion and all other methods and means of checking the mighty tide of intemperance have practically passed out of the people's mind. But how are we going to secure the suffrage of the people favoring prohibition? Ah! that is the question of questions to-day. And another question in this connection naturally intrudes itself upon our mind for answer. It is, How speedily can this great moral reform be accomplished? We will answer you the first question: How can we secure the suffrage of the people favoring prohibition? I know of no other way; I know of no other course in which to turn my eyes for a ray or gleam of hope, but the one I have mentioned in preceding lectures. It is to educate and Christianize the people of our Nation, especially the young men and rising generation, and imbue and instill into their minds temperance principles.

You say that is a slow and tedious process, true it is, but there is no other practical way. You cannot pass prohibitory laws in this State—of Kentucky—at the present time or at the next State election. Why, the answer is very simple; public sentiment is not ready for it; and does not favor it. And if you should put prohibitory laws upon your statute books to-morrow, you could not enforce them in this State. Why? because public sentiment and public opinion would not sustain the officers of the law and efforts would prove futile. You can give this State all the way from one to three decades of years upon the prohibition question. While in some States prohibition has already been accomplished, or may be accomplished at the next State election. You ask, why this difference between States? I answer it is owing to the difference in the advancement and progress of moral, intellectual and religious culture. There is a difference in educational facilities, and in moral and intellectual culture in some of the Northern States. And the same is also true of some of the Southern States. Besides in some States prohibition is more practical and accessible for other reasons. In some States there is no organized whisky interests or corporation to contend with, and in other States there is, notably in this State. This State is not ready for prohibition. And to my mind it seems decidedly clownish for a man to run for an office upon the prohibition ticket; or champion a distinctive, prohibition, political party. A distinctive temperance, prohibition party is about as likely to control the affairs of this Nation as a gnat upon the bosom of the ocean is to control its tides.

This great moral reform which the people of this country have in view, and at heart, cannot be accomplished by such spasmodic efforts. We are dependent upon the progress of Christian civilization to accomplish this work of reformation. We are dependent upon an enlightened Christian sentiment to cope with and overcome the evil of intemperance. If we had a stronger

Christian sentiment among the people, we could effect the suppression of the liquor traffic by Legislation. But we have not got that Christian sentiment and consequently we must wait until we can develop it. The religion of our Lord Jesus Christ is the great living, vital, moving, conserving power that is to effect the reformation of the world in the matter of intemperance and in every other respect. And, inasmuch as a moral or religious sentiment is involved in the Legislation against the liquor traffic, inasmuch as prohibition is a political measure springing from moral impulses, we will have an opportunity of observing that the improvement of the prospects favoring its accomplishment will be commensurate with the development of religious sentiment.

We talk about temperance societies and organizations carrying through this great work. They simply cannot do it. As I have said, they are but the dashing waves upon the bosom, while the religion of Christ upon which the Church is established is the great undertone and undercurrent of the sea ; and it is abundantly able to buoy up and float any vessel of reform you may launch upon its crested waves and crystal tide. The Christian communities of this great country, in which the Church of the living God is centered, and from which it has sprung is—infinitely more than temperance societies—the stronghold and bulwark of temperance reform movements. And it is from this Divine source we must look for help and strength in accomplishing the work in hand. Let us then strengthen the arms of the Church, and encourage educational interests, that from these sources we may derive the help needful when the crisis comes in the work of this great moral reform. May we look toward Heaven for light to guide our feet, and may God clear our vision and crown our labors with well deserved triumph.

Temperance a Religio-Political Issue.

question paramount in the minds of the people of this country to-day is, shall the liquor question, as a moral issue, enter the domain of National politics? Which is about equivalent to asking, if moral and religious questions shall be made an issue in the politics of this country? And if this question is answered in the affirmative, and if, when this issue is tested it is decided in the affirmative, then have we not got—at least practically—a Union of church and State.

The question is great in magnitude, complex in character, and is well worth probing. It is a question that has not been settled, but one that is coming up for settlement. It is a question so tremendous and far reaching, that it bids fair to shake the foundation of our civil Government, and put to a crucial test Republicanism involving the fate and destiny of the institutions of free Government. The question of "questions" in this age is, have moral or religious issues a place in the domain of politics or National Government? Would that we could settle this issue. But this issue or question is to be settled in the ages to come, and that too by the controlling suffrage element of society in this country. This question has sprung up out of, and is peculiar to the Christian civilization of the American people. The settlement of the Sunday question and the liquor traffic—and these questions are twins—will shake the very foundation of American society, and move the principalities and powers of this grand American Nation.

We can discuss some of the favorable and unfavorable points in this great question in a single lecture, or in a brief pamphlet, and settle this question, perhaps, so far as we are individually concerned; but we cannot settle it for this expansive Nation. This question must go before the people in various ways, and eventually and finally be settled by the masses at the ballot-box, from whose stern arbitrament there is no appeal, whose voice and whose ruling is the supreme law of the land and the strength of our National Government. In this country we get the chrystalized opinion or senses of the people at the ballot-box on political questions; and I have sometimes almost dared to wish that we had a pure Democracy, rather than a Representative Democracy, so that all questions might go more speedily and directly before the people for settlement. I apprehend that if this was the case we would get a constitutional amendment favoring prohibition much more speedily than we will be able to get it by the round about way and tedious process by which we are at present endeavoring to secure such national legislation.

The people of this country are habituated to the practice of settling political questions and issues by the ballot. One hundred, yes one thousand times within the history of this Government have purely political issues been irrevocably settled at the ballot box. The people of this country are not slow in taking political issues by the horns. They have the moral courage, and they have the intellectual qualifications for grasping political issues and measures that have a bearing upon the interest and welfare of the country. But the liquor question and the Sunday question, at least as yet have not become generally known and generally conceded as purely political measures. They have heretofore been considered or classed as moral or religious questions rather than political questions. And for this reason there has been a hesitancy and an indifference on the part of the people in acting upon them. It has never been quite clear to the minds of the people, and as yet it is not quite clear, that these questions of such sacred character and such sublime import should be thrust into the domain of politics. And the people have been waiting for light upon these questions. They have been waiting for evolution and for development along this line, that they might see more clearly along an unknown way. The temperance issue is a moral issue. Now the question is, shall we take moral or religious issues into the domain of politics? Shall we resort to a political tribunal for judgment upon a purely moral or religious question? The people of this country are less fully committed upon this question than upon any other question that disturbs the minds of this Nation of Sovereigns.

I am convinced that some men favor legal prohibition who have no intelligent conception of the fact that by so doing they are in a measure favoring a blending of religion and politics, or, in other words, favoring a union of Church and State. Prohibition is a moral issue. It is defended upon moral grounds and upon moral principles. The adherents and champions of legal prohibition press this issue forward because intemperance is wrong; because it has an immoral, degrading and enslaving tendency; and not because there is anything unjust about the custom of intemperance and the sale of liquor. If there was a manifest injustice in the liquor traffic to the individual or to the National Government, then it might be pressed as a purely political issue. It is all that and more too. But that is not the motive and not the reason why legal prohibition is agitated to-day, and pressed forward for speedy accomplishment.— But the reason why it is agitated to-day is, that the liquor traffic is inhuman; that it is harmful, degrading and demoralizing to the individual and to the Nation.

This measure of legal prohibition had its birth in the heart of christian men and philanthropist. It springs from humane motives and christian impulses, and but few of the friends of temperance ever stopped to consider the question, whether the liquor traffic does an actual injustice to the individual or to the Nation. This is conceded by them, but they do not press the issue of prohibition upon the plea or grounds of injustice, but upon the grounds of immorality and inhumanity; therefore legal prohibition in a proper and in a very true sense is a moral and not a physical or political issue. It certainly is not a political issue in the sense that the tariff or banking systems are political issues. These great questions are pressed forward as political issues upon the grounds of equity and justice, and not because of any moral or humane principle or quality that attaches to them. They are purely physical issues, financial in their character and without any particular moral significance; but the question of legal prohibition is the reverse of all these, it is purely a moral or religious question, and it is for this reason that the people have a hesitancy in pressing prohibition measures forward as a political issue. They look at the tendency and possible outcome and then shrink back, for if the destruction and extermination of the liquor traffic is prompted and inspired from humane moral or religious motives, then the prohibition issue savors with a blending of religion and politics, or a union of church and State, and there is among our people a prejudice as deep and fathomless as the emotions of mens souls against religious questions entering the domain of politics.

But while men are quibbling over this distinction and carefully considering this point, let them not forget that the liquor traffic is no more a distinctive, moral or religious question, than was the slave trade. The slavery question was agitated and pressed forward as a political issue until it shook the very foundation of our National Government, because it was wrong, immoral and inhuman, and not because the trade inflicted an injustice upon our Government in any way. The anti-slavery controversy had its birth and origin in the hearts of Christian men and philanthropist far back in the century. So we are confronted again at this point with the momentious question, shall or shall not moral or religious questions or questions springing from such sources enter the domain of politics; and in so doing become pillars in the structure of our National Government; giving the constitution of our Government a religious complexion. And in discussing this question, I shall do so from the standpoint that the temperance question is purely a moral or religious question, and is pressed forward as a political issue because of its moral or religious tendency, character and import.

It seems to me that it does not take a man of supernatural intelligence to understand and to comprehend the fact that prohibition is purely a moral issue and has a religious bearing and significance. Well, what of it? Suppose it is. Suppose it is purely a religious question ; what difference does that make? Now this is the point we wish to discuss. We will determine what difference it makes. We will see whether the people of this country favor National Legislation upon religious questions, as well as upon purely political questions.

As we have stated, there is a deep-seated prejudice among the people of this country against anything that smacks of State religion. Our people shrink with a devout horror from the thought of a union of Church and State. And I apprehend that if it was generally believed that a constitutional amendment suppressing the traffic of strong drink was the initial step leading to the ultimate union of Church and State, it would eclipse in everlasting darkness every ray of hope of accomplishing legal prohibition. But to my mind this is the plausible and evident meaning of legislative prohibition. Men generally will not accept this as a fact, or even as a rational theory or view. But have those

who question and doubt the validity and rationality of the theory or view
touching the union of Church and State, studied carefully and fathomed in
thought the nature, character, purpose and magnitude of Christ's kingdom on
earth? Do they believe in the universal spread and dominion of Christ's
kingdom from the "rising to the setting of the sun?" Do they comprehend
the fact that the nature and design of Christ's kingdom—by which is meant
the Christian religion—is to dominate the whole world, and bring the whole
world under subjection to it? That Christ's kingdom is to come upon earth,
and his will is to be done on earth as it is in heaven? Do they realize the fact
that every instrumentality, influence and power in this world is to be overruled
for his glory, and is to be used in the great battle of "Armageddon," in which
the world is to be conquered and brought under the dominion of Christ? This
is the sure word of prophecy, and in some way or other—in a way perhaps not
yet altogether clear even to the Christian world—this thing is to come to pass.
For Christ's kingdom is to be established in the earth, and the "kingdoms of
this world are to become his kingdom," and He is to be enthroned King over
all. This marvelous drama of Events is as sure to come to pass as the sun is
to rise in its beauty, and light up the universe, on the coming morrow.

The Christian world is divided as to how Christ's Kingdom is to come or
to be established. But, however that may be, it must be clearly evident to
any thoughtful mind, that this world is ripening for some great event; and that
we are crossing the threshold of a day of wonderful grandeur and triumph.
To the thoughtful Christian mind the marvelous inventions of the nineteenth
century and of the last three centuries have a wonderful significance and sacred
meaning as they stand related to the religion of Christ. Take the printing press,
the telegraph, the railroad, the steamship, the telephone and a thousand other
inventions; and to the Christian man they have a peculiar and sacred meaning, from what they have to the worldly-minded man. To the Christian mind
these things are simply auxiliaries and helps to assist and aid in the promotion,
advancement and establishment of Christ's Kingdom upon earth. These
wonderful inventions, you will observe, did not crop out away back in the
mediæval ages and the dark ages of the world's history, but as if by a Divine
hand they were kept back, and in abeyance, for this golden and resplendent
age of reformation and enlightenment. It may be asked why is this? I am
not certain that I can answer, but the best reason that can be given, is the
one already intimated that this world and its progressive unfolding is under
the supervision of God, and that he is overruling all things for his own glory
and for the interests of Christ's Kingdom; that it was His design and His
hand that kept in abeyance these wonderful inventions until the sunlight of
the day of reformation broke in resplendent beauty and glory upon the world.

One thing Christians build hope upon, as upon a rock; and that is the
prophecy that the Kingdom of God is coming upon earth, and that His will
shall be done here as it is in Heaven. The general belief is that this triumph
of Christ's cause and kingdom is to come by evolution; by a gradual and progressive development and unfolding until the whole world shall be spiritualized
and Christianized. If these things are true, and are admitted to be true, then
it certainly is also true that God will overrule and bring into use every instru-

mentality, power and influence upon earth for the accomplishment of this purpose and end. And certainly is it true that if the mighty inventions, powers and instrumentalities of this nineteenth century were more wholly consecrated to the work and service of the Divine Master, as they are now partially consecrated—they would hasten rapidly the coming of the Kingdom of Christ. What are some of these instrumentalities of which we are speaking? You will probably suggest the printing press; and it has proven a mighty power and agency in advancing the interest of the Redeemer's Kingdom. And I in turn would suggest that political parties or organizations are or may become powerful instrumentalities in assisting and carrying on to completion the work of the Redeemer's Kingdom. When a man becomes a Christian, everything he has and is, is consecrated to Christ, and given to Him. And is it not equally true, that when a Nation becomes Christianized, that everything that belongs to it will be consecrated to Christ. Now, this is what I mean by what has already been said. When a Nation becomes thoroughly Christian, then its wealth, its merchandise, its lands, its institutions of learning, its political organizations and machinery of human Government, everything that it has will be consecrated to Christ and brought into use in establishing and maintaining His Kingdom.

When we come to more intelligently understand the nature and character of Christ's mission and kingdom among men, we will realize that there is no instrumentality or agency in the world that may not, with all due reverence and propriety, be consecrated to the work of His kingdom. Now I have pursued this line of argument thus far, with the faint hope of showing the plausibility and rationality of a union of Church and State. I know of no valid reason why the Christian people of this Nation, or any nation, if they have the supremacy of power, may not join hands and organize a political party and promote by legislation the interests of Christ's kingdom upon earth. And I would ask you, if you know of any valid reason why this thing should not be done? I believe this is the tendency and drift of human affairs. It may be looking forward to an ideal age or period in the world's history, and we may not see much of it in our time, but in the ages to come I believe everything— every instrumentality and agency, even to the inclusion of political parties—will be made sacred by reason of their consecration to the interest and advancement of Christ's kingdom upon earth. It is in this sense I speak of a union of Church and State. But we are accustomed to look upon political parties as about the most corrupt thing in the world. Well, what is the remedy? Extermination? That cannot be done. We cannot run human governments without them. There is a better remedy. It is for the nine millions of Christian people in this country to make their voice heard and their influence felt in the legislation and in the political affairs of the Nation. The only rescue of this Nation from corruption must come from this source.. What have we to-day in the political and national affairs of this Republic? We have Christless statesmen, Christless Legislatures, a Christless Congress, a Christless Senate, a Christless President, a Christless Constitution. I am not in sympathy with the flagrant charge that corruption is rampant in our national affairs, but I do claim that Christ should not be ruled out of our Government and out of the affairs

of our Nation. Directly and specifically the Christian people have no voice or
representation in the affairs of our National Government. It is a startling
thought and a thrilling commentary upon the religious age and upon this religious country, that in our National Congress there is not to be found one
individual Christian statesman; that neither in the Senate nor in the House
of Representatives is there to be found a Christian, or at least a spiritual-
minded man, according to the true and intrinsic meaning of that term. You
may find an exceptional case, but if so, it only proves the rule. This is a
Christian age, and perhaps the golden age of the world's history, but in all the
realm of enlightened America, North, South, East or West, can you put your
finger upon a Christian Statesman. We have had such men. The Christian
people of this country have not forgotten the imperishable memory of such
christian men as Washington, Adams, Lincoln, and Wilson; but statesmen
who believe in Christ and acknowledge him as their Saviour and the Saviour of
the world are painfully scarce in this memorable epoch and decade of our
Nation's history.

Now I am satisfied that things will not always be thus, that in the near
future the christian people of our county will unite their voices and claim a
representation not only for themselves—but a representation for Christ in the
political affairs of this grand Christian Nation, and after while when the christian religion has gained greater strength it will have, and claim, a controlling
voice in the legislation and in the ruling of this great commonwealth and republic. If that day should ever come to pass when a religious political party
shall rule this nation, will we not have then a union of church and State?
Bring the national affairs of our county under the control of a religious political
organization or party and we practically have a union of church and State.
Well what of it? Suppose we have a State religion, would any harm necessarily spring from such a source? Well that depends altogether upon the character of the religion. It depends upon whether it be the christian religion or
some other religion. I admit that if a religion is to be recognized by the
State that it makes a world of difference as to what religion it is. There is
but one true religion, and that is the christian religion, but there is Mormonism,
there is Priestcraft, there is Budhism, Mohamodanism and a thousand other
forms of false and idolatrous religions. Now I believe that the religion of
Christ in all its sweetness, purity and loveliness of character might be safely
and advantageously recognized by the State and blended with the affairs of
Government; whereas any of the other forms of religion thus recognized or
blended would prove degrading, demoralizing and disastrious to the interest of
political Government.

The most of men we meet have a holy horror of the very thought of a
State religion, and manifest a vicious repugnance at the mention of such a
proposition, and if such a measure should be introduced in our national Congress I am convinced that there would be frightful consternation, if not an in-
suppressible stampede in the ranks of our "christian Statesmen." The people of
this land, the masses we meet, have what passes for conviction upon this great
subject, it is that the proposition of a State religion is intolerable, insufferable,
and at once inimical to the wishes of the people and to the interest of the

country. But what do the masses of the country know either practically or theoretically about the tendency, effects or results of a Union of Church and State? They know—and I speak with due consideration for peoples convictions—they know about as much upon the subject as the hooting owls of the forest know about it. If they know anything at all it is what they have gleaned from the history of past ages. But some one asks, is not the past history of the world a valuable legacy, and shall not we profit by the past experience of the race? I answer in a limited sense that is true. It is true only when the circumstances involved are similar, and the cases parallel.

The most of men who have thoughts or views upon this subject of a Union of Church and State, draw their illustration, their examples, their inferences, their conviction and their prejudices, from the failures and disasters along this line, dating far back in the history of the centuries. They go back in history to the mediæval ages and find examples and illustrations of the disastrous, pernicious and cruel results and workings of a State religion, and hold that up before the world as a criterion, and as an illustration of what will follow if we establish a State religion. But the illustration does not prove anything, because the cases are not parallel. We cannot without deep emotions and tears of pity read of the idolatrous customs practiced by oriental Nations and sanctioned by their Governments. And we revolt and turn with mutterings of anguish upon our lips from reading of the inquisition and the wanton cruel and bloody sacrifice of the lives of fifty millions of Christians by the Romish Church, while sustained and sanctioned by the temporal powers and kingdoms of Europe. It is from these sources we get our illustrations and examples of the pernicious, disastrous and fateful results flowing from a Union of Church and State.

It is from these sources that men have got a prejudice against a State religion that runs as deep as the emotions of their soul. But after all, this prejudice is not justly founded, for the cases are not parallel. I tell you, it makes a world of difference, whether the State religion be the religion of idolatry, from which springs the worship of graven images, and the cruel tortures and sacrifices of human beings, or whether it be the Christian religion. It makes a world of difference whether the State religion be the dominating Priestcraft of a Romish hierarchy, or whether it be the pure, gentle and blessed religion of our Lord Jesus Christ. Because the designing and vicious Romish hierarchy, with its venomous talons, clutched the mighty empires of Europe, and made them a prey to its lustful passions, dragging them down into reproach, degradation and ruin; because of this, it does not follow that the holy and blessed religion of Christ, purified from every breath and taint of sin and selfishness, may not be blended and woven with the very warp and woof of the fabric of the constitution of our National Government, and that with signally blessed purifying and elevating results, rather than with pernicious and disastrous consequences.

The experiment of blending Church and State has not been tried in modern times; and the views that men generally entertain upon this subject are Pagan rather than Christian. What we are as a Nation of people, politically, intellectually and in every other respect—and we have the grandest

Nation on earth—is attributable to the humanizing, ameliorating and elevating inflences of the Christian religion upon our civilization. And sublimely true is it, that true religion elevates and enobles a nation rather than degrades and destroys it. Take the Bible history of the rise and fall of the Patriarchal empires and kingdoms, and they are among the grandest of which history relates; and you will find that God himself established them and chose their Kings and Rulers; that they were under His supervision, that He was the counsellor of their Kings; that the Kings communed with Him and talked with Him face to face, receiving instructions and Divine guidance touching the management and rule of their mighty kingdoms. And what is more, you will observe that it was only when those ancient Kings disobeyed the voice of God, and departed from his instructions and fell into idolatry and sin, that their kingdoms came crashing down in ruins upon their heads.

There is another illustration that comes to my mind, and it is peculiarly beautiful and precious. It is that the inspired writers in their prophesies of future events frequently ventured the prediction, that at Christ's coming again to earth, the "kingdoms of this world shall become His kingdoms."— That He will re-establish the throne of David and rule the Nations of earth. It seems to me that the central thought of the prophecy touching the second advent of the Savior is that when He comes again, it will be to take into His own hand the sceptre of the Kings of earth, and exalt to thrones and rule the nations of earth. Christ Himself put the prophecy on record, and this will be His crowning achievement upon earth. This prophecy, some say, has a spiritual meaning and significance. It may, or it may not. But however that may be, I am convinced that if ever a time comes when there is to be a millennium of universal peace upon earth, and the kingdoms of earth are to be united and the world is to be ruled by one King, that that King will be Christ, the crucified Nazarine. And I am convinced that even now, Christ desires and covets an interest, a representation and a controlling influence in the management of the political affairs of governments and nations, that He may use legislation, as well as the printing press to His glory and for the advancement of His Kingdom upon earth. And I believe the Christian people of America will soon wake up to the realization of this eternally sublime truth.

Now to the world and especially to the infidel class the things about which we have been talking are as an idle tale and unworthy of credence. I cannot help that, but let me tell you that my estimate of infidelity is that it is human drollery, that if we cannot believe the sacred story of Christ as the Savior of the world and of his return again to redeem the whole world to himself, then the ground breaks through beneath our feet, and we have no foundation upon which to stand.

But let us pursue this thought touching the blending of religion and patriotism for another moment. Among the best element of christians you will often hear men exhorting their fellow men to take their religion with them into their business, to manifest and exhibit it there in the commercial transactions of life, to preach the living Christ by example, by action, by word and precept. This is commendable, it is the right and proper thing for a christian man to do, and we ask is it not as rational, and can we not with the same propriety and commendation take our religion into our politics with us? Is not the same principle involved in either case? The actual difference between the two propositions is not worthy of discussion. Christian men at the ballot box should show their preference for Christian candidates for office, and influenced by religious motives, they should make a wise selection in the choice of political parties. If there is a party in the field that has a religious leaning, bearing or tendency, that is the party the christian man should support by his suffrage. There is a difference between political parties, they should not be indiscriminately censured and held up to ridicule and contempt.

General Garfield told us that "partizanship is opinion crystalized, and party organizations are the scaffolding whereon citizens stand while they build up the walls of their national temple." Organizations he said, "may change or dissolve, but when political parties cease to exist, liberty will perish." It seems to me that the grandest exhibition of loyalty to Christ and to the interest of His Kingdom is found in a faithful interest in and devotion to the development and perpetuity of National free Government, by a wise and conservative use of suffrage rights and power. The christian people of this country will yet more fully awake to the realization of this grand truth, and in the near future we will witness an exhibition of the hand of the Church in the management of the political affairs of our Government.

This is the truth I have labored to present. And when the time comes, when the Christian suffrage element of the people, are empowered with a controlling influence and voice in the management of the political affairs of the country, and righteous men shall execute righteous laws, then will we understand more fully the sympathies and blending harmonies of patriotism and religion. And when in the course of human events, the laws of our land shall be enacted and administered by Christian men, then will we not have essentially an Union of Church and State? If this character or order of Union of Church and States comes to pass, it will come as a matter of destiny or as a Divine providence. It will come in the Divine order of things. It will come as a natural sequence, it will come inevitably. It will come to pass without the co-operation or aid of men. It will come whether men will it or not, it will come despite their prejudices, or in the face of hostile opposition. The Union of Church and State of which I speak will come as a revolution. And revolutions come with the power of a whirlwind. Revolutions come with a bound, and are never known to reverse their course. And the will of man or of a combination of men cannot resist it.

During the dark days of the rebellion when our continent rocked beneath the tread of marching armies, and men were being destroyed by the iron hail of battle, an old lady in the State of Missouri, who had pondered over the subject, was heard to remark that "no one man could stop the war." She said "her husband went to Washington for that purpose, but all to no avail." So in the matter of reform measures or revolutions that have a Divine mission or character, they are destined to work out their course and the will of no individual man, nor of the whole world can change the current of the movement. And I repeat and emphasize this, the inmost conviction of my life, that this greatest of revolutions in the affairs of men and of Nations, viz: The harmonizing, the blending and the unification of religion and patriotism is well on the way. And I aver as a truth that cannot be shaken or overturned, that no harm or danger can spring from a blending of or weaving into the very texture and fabric of our constitution and of the political affairs of our Nation anything so transcendently pure, elevating and enobling as the Christian religion.

But why this lengthy argument upon this subject? It is this: I believe in a union of Church and State, and offer this argument as a justification for my belief, because I recognize that temperance legislation is Christian legislation; that it is a master-stroke of policy for the advancement of Christ's kingdom. And when that is done, what may we not expect will follow? We may then expect a constitutional amendment for the protection of the holy Sabbath day. And then following closely upon the heels of that a constitutional amendment recognizing the Christian religion. And when these things come to pass we will have practically and essentially a union of Church and State. And when I calmly contemplate the steady spread, growth, power, and wide encircling influence of the Church, I am convinced that this result will speedily and inevitably be reached. This is the inevitable tendency and drift of the centralized power of the Church. And there is no combined power or influence upon earth that can check the current of this swift tide or change its course. Back of the Church is an invincible army of God-fearing men, and back of the Church is the will and impulse of God, who "knows no variableness nor the shadow of turning."

The time, I apprehend, will soon come in the history of this country when the Congress and Senate of our Nation will obey the behest of the Church, and statesmen will gladly do the bidding and bend to the will of a God-fearing and God-serving constituency. The time, I believe, is swiftly approaching when a religious character will be an essential qualification for the high and honored office of a Congressman or a Senator, and Infidel and free-thinking statesmen will give way to Christian statesmen, who, in the fear and in the love of God, will make and enact the laws of a Christian people and a Christian Nation. It is from this source and through this channel we must look for help in this great political issue of temperance reform. And whether the temperance reform is a religious question or not, it is certainly true that it is so nearly a religious question that no temperance legislation can be secured until we have more of a religious complexion in the Legislatures of our States and in the Congress of our Nation. Some one may be heard to say, religion has nothing to do with the question in hand. That may be his convictions, but it is certainly true that we cannot leave the Christian religion out of the question and accomplish the desired results, namely, temperance legislation.

There are those who have no defined religious or political views or preferences who venture the worse than effeminate belief, that the temperance problem will be taken up by the people and settled by them independent of religious creeds or political parties. This belief or view is simply maudlin, and a gross exhibition of stupidity; for all legislative measures or constitutional amendments are necessarily, essentially and always political issues. Among a people where the ballot is the sovereign arbiter, the only possible means of settling national questions is by making them political issues. The question in hand, the question of national temperance reform, must necessarilly become a political issue. And it is destined to make an exceedingly lively one. Personally, I have confidence in Republicanism. It is my faith that the grand mission, and, I may say, the sacred mission of the Republican party is, or will be, to take up the great issue of national temperance reform, and bear it upon its stalwart shoulders to ultimate and decisive victory. I have but little preference as to which of the two great political parties—great at least numerically—of this country shall accomplish this great political reform.

I am confident however that the Democratic party has no affinities for the temperance reform movement, and will strictly oppose legislation along this line. It would indeed be an amusing scene to witness the Democratic party championing temperance legislation or any reform movement. It is settled beyond peradventure, to my mind that the great and decisive battle for temperance reform will have to be fought by the Republican party, and in due time it will champion the work that the friends of temperance have mapped out, and carry it on to completion. It will not make undue and unwise haste in the matter and attempt more than it can perform. I am not in favor of pressing prohibition as a political issue, where it jeopardizes or pressages the defeat of the Republican party. The achievement of prohibitory legislation is preeminently desirable, but to me individually, the grand history and sacred memory of the Republican party is of greater importance than the immediate destruction of the liquor traffic. As ardently as I love temperance principles I would not favor pressing prohibition forward as a political issue under circumstance or contingencies calculated to jeopardize or imperil the interest of the Republican political organization.

It is important to counsel conservative views upon the propriety of hastily pushing prohibition forward as a political question; especially in States that are not ready for the issue, and where there is nothing to be gained. It is the extreme of folly to overburden a political party by putting upon it more than it can carry; thereby breaking it down and inflicting irreparable injury. The centuries are before us, and there is plenty of time yet in which to settle the temperance question. It is a question to be settled in the ages to come. And in fact it is not morally certain that prohibition by legislation is practical or possible. It is an undertaking that extends further into the future than we can see. At least, whatever our confidence may be, it cannot go beyond this, that the fate of the temperance cause is involved in the advance movement of Christian civilization. One is identical with the other. The fate of one is involved in the fate of the other. And it will take the concentrated action of every influence that is in sympathy with the philanthropic and Divine work of ennobling, elevating and Christianizing fallen humanity to effect a permanent National temperance reformation through political power or influence.

But whether the prospects of victory be immediate or far distant, the work must not stop. The interest of our free Christian Nation must be subserved. It demands the abolition of the accurse liquor traffic. It is the function of National Government to protect its own interest, and to defend its own life. The Rum Demon has clutched our Nation by the throat, and in the throes of death it cries out for help and rescue from concentrated political action, that its life may be spared and the treasonable foe destroyed. It will put to a crucial test the political power of this Nation to do this. It is from this source we are to expect relief and rescue. It is political action or it is National putrifaction, disintegration and death. Ministers have been known to say that the church will manage the temperance question, and that the church is a temperance organization. That is all true enough, but the dainty temperance sermons we hear occasionally from the pulpit; will not materially affect the mighty current of the work of intemperance. It will require something more powerful than this. It has got to be made a distinctive, political issue, and then the church or at least the Christian people of this country have got to take it up and bear it on to victory.

The temperance question has got to be handled as slavery was handled—as a distinctively political issue. If this temperance question is left alone for the Church to settle and dispose of,—it is not certainly known but that it may in a measure turn around and defend the criminal traffic rather than attempt to destroy it. When slavery was in full blast in this country ministers of the gospel were found defending the accursed institution, and vainly endeavoring to prove by the Bible that human slavery had a right to exist, and alas, politicians sought to make the constitution of this country defend and protect slavery, but slavery slipped out. As a political issue we found a solution to the problem of slavery, and only as a political issue could it have been settled. So I apprehend this liquor traffic will never be settled until our National Congress sweeps down upon it with the avalanche of a constitutional amendment Mild assuasive temperance sermons will neither check or destroy the evil of intemperance. It will take a political tornado sweeping with irresistable and devastating power over the broad domain of this Nation to destroy forever this accursed evil.

Men say that in the matter of eating and drinking the people should do as they please; that it is neither the province nor the function of Governmen to meddle or interfere with the personal liberty of men in this respect.— This is all very well as an argument, but it is not a theory or foundation principle upon which we can with any degree of safety build the grand structure of free Government. We have practically tried and tested this theory in free America, and what is the result? The result is a motley civilization. We have in America developed a Christian civilization and a religious zeal as pure —it seems to me—as the breath of the eternal morning. We have also developed a class of men and women who, if isolated from Christian communities, might very properly and justly be denominated "a nation of drunkards." In the midst of Christian people, and under the shadow of church spires, the American saloon has bred a civilization that fosters crime and brutality, that desecrates the holy Sabbath day, and seeks to trample beneath its, already, blood-stained feet everything sacred, pure and holy.

We have tried in Christian America the practice of giving men the liberty to drink as much as they want of whatever they please, and the result has been disastrous to the development and progressive march of Christian civilization, as well as disastrous to the best interest of the country in every respect. We have tried the practice of selling fiery beverages that madden the brain, inflame the passions, and incite murder, crime and insanity; and we find that, as the twilight rays of the evening of a long century falls upon us, our civilization has been marred, and that the moral, intellectual, and physical development and growth of the Nation has been retarded and obstructed. We have a license law which, ostensibly, has for its purpose the limiting or restraining of the custom of drinking these fiery beverages; but it virtually serves no other purpose than to make drinking more expensive. It is in no sense and to no extent a restraint, and in the face of it America has, or is fast becoming a Nation of besotted drunkards. Drunkenness is rampant in this country to-day. Men with vicious, brutal passions, fired by the burning, flaming beverages of hell, are every day committing crimes as red as crimson, or black as the shadows of the infernal abyss.

If I should pause here to tell you of the wreck and ruin of drinking in the homes of America, to call over the category of crimes and aggregate the extent and character of the suffering, wretchedness, poverty and woe that spring directly from this source of strong drink alone, I would horrify you. Your sensitive minds and hearts would shrink and recoil with dismay and terror from the recital of such a damning record of guilt and crime, and you would marvel that such things should exist, or that they should come to pass in this free, enlightened Christian country, of which we are justly proud. If these things are true then shall we not, in the name of humanity and in the name of God who reigns in heaven, lay hold of this practice of drinking strong drink?—And whether it be a moral or physical, religious or political question, make it a national campaign issue, and by the crystallized power of the ballot destroy the accursed traffic from out our land, that our Nation may be indeed a free Nation, and our country be redeemed for Christ the Eternal King!

Political and the Religious Phases of the Temperance Issue.

ACRED history tells us that after man's creation, which was but a little lower than that of angels, he not only sinned and fell from his high estate, but that morally and intellectually he sank down until he became an heathen, even an idolator, worshiping false gods. And when Christ was upon earth, at the beginning of the Christian era, we find civilization at a very low ebb, and the plight and condition of the race of mankind sad and pitiable. And not until we pass through the mediæval and dark ages, and come to the sixteenth century, do we see any change for the better, or any improvement in the condition of the race. The light of heaven then dawned upon the world. The reformation began and swept every thing before it. A Christian civilization sprang up, unlike anything that had ever been witnessed in the centuries of the past. This Christian civilization has been moving on as the breath of a mighty tempest, destroying by its irresistible sweep every relic of Paganism and of the dark ages, and paving the way for better things to come.

In the wake of Christian civilization has followed intemperance, developing with the ages and becoming more formidable and distressing than was ever known during any period of the world's history. It is a little strange that in this age of enlightenment, and in those nations that are most fully developed, where the religion of Christ has become the standard religion, and education is ample and universal, and progress and improvement is written upon the face of the work of man's hands every where—it is a little strange that under the auspicious circumstances which we have mentioned that intemperance and drunkenness should become rank and rife, sweeping over the land with the destructiveness of a mighty deluge. It is a little strange that in this high noon of the nineteenth century, when Christianity and Christian civilization is the boast of our Nation and of the world, that intemperance and the universally pervailing custom of the excessive use of intoxicating liquors should become so distressing and destructive to human happiness and human life, that it becomes necessary to consider the importance of legislating against the manufacture, importation and sale of strong drink, and by legislation banish the traffic from within the bounds of our Christian land and free Nation. We take a retrospect of the world's history, and we do not find that at any time or period intemperance was so abounding and destructive that it was considered necessary to suppress the use of strong drink and intoxicating beverages by legislation or by the majesty of the law. It is only as we come down to this present age of civil liberty and intellectual culture, to the very close of this glowing nineteenth century, that the terrible ravages of strong drink and intemperance makes it obligatory and imperative upon us to restrain and to crush this evil by Legislation.

There is one thought at this point of peculiar interest. It is this; we have said that in tracing the history of the world down from the earliest dawn until we approach the nineteenth century, that there never was a period when drunkenness and the excessive use of wine or strong drink was so prevalent and used so excessively that its use made it a pest and a scourge, so that national prohibition measures or laws were enacted or enforced against it by any Nation. The race of mankind all down through the ages was temperate, at least temperate compared with what it is now. And here is the thought of special interest : Had it occurred that any nation at any time during the past history of the world, had been attacked or besieged by drunkenness, so much so that its national life and existence had been threatened by the scourge; I say if this thing of which I have spoken had occurred, it is a remarkable truth that that Nation, whatever Nation it might have been, would not have had the moral strength and moral courage to oppose, to combat, to crush the evil that threatened its existence.

Review the history of the Nation of the earth during the past ages, and you will find that they were so feeble and impotent morally and intellectually, so destitute of practical intelligence, moral strength and courage, that had intemperance and drunkenness attacked them as viciously as it has attacked some of the Nations of the world in this present age, that it would or might have swept them out of existence, depopulating and devastating their territory, and the people would not have had the moral power, strength and wisdom to have confronted, combated and destroyed the evil. But rather the evil would have destroyed them, root and branch. This is not idle speculation, but a remarkable fact. Intemperance never viciously attacked any of the Nations in other ages or in the past ages of the world's history; but its attack was reserved —as it were by an unseen providence—for this age of Christian enlightenment and civil liberty. Not until this closing half of the nineteenth century has it attacked and besieged the Nations of earth with frightful ravages and devastating terror. And even to-day its greatest work of devastatation of ruin and of death, is confined to Great Britain and America, two of the most advanced and enlightened Christian Nations of earth. I ask is this not literally true; and if true is it not very remarkable? How providentially strange it it, that intemperance in its most frightful character should attack only those Nations, and only in an age, when those Nations are best qualified and most nearly capable of grappling with the evil, resisting its advances, and crushing it as a destructive foe.

I marvel at this truth, that only in this country and in this age of the worlds history, has intemperance and its work of ruin been so rank and rife and so malignant in its character that it has become necessary and imperative to consider the importance of enacting and enforcing a national Legislative law against the manufacture and sale of strong drink; and it seems providentially fortunate that the reign of rum drinking and drunkenness should sway its sceptre over this Nation just at a time when it is best prepared and equipped to cope with and to overcome this giant towering evil. The moral strength of our country is at its best. The intellectual force and religious zeal of the people of this Nation is a match for any foe to the christian civilization of this country. These mighty influences are capable of resisting the strides of drunkenness in America; and it is this Nation more perhaps than any other with the exception of Great Britain that is menaced by the liquor traffic. America and Great Britain are the greatest Nations of drunkards in the world to-day, and these Nations have the greatest moral strength of any Nations to grapple with and destroy this pestilential scourge of intemperance.

The liquor traffic and the disastrous results it entails upon the race, viewed in the most charitable light is a menace to Christian civilization, and a menace to our free institution of Republican Government. The rum traffic is grappling at the throat of our Government. It is corrupting the ballot-box, bribing votes, and controlling political elections, wherever it has a controlling influence. In round numbers one billion of dollars are invested in the liquor traffic, and half a million of men are engaged in the destructive enterprise; and there is scarcely a township, county or State election in which the mighty power and influence of this damning traffic is not felt, and in many cases it shapes and controls the elections. In a very broad and terrible sense is it true that the liquor traffic is a menace to our institution of free Government; and its encroachment must be resisted by the moral strength and impulse of the Nation. Intemperance has come as a battering ram against the stately pillars of our national temple, threatening with downfall and destruction the grandest structure ever reared by mortal hands. But the brave and trusted hands that reared this grand temple are abundantly able to protect and defend it from the ruthless attacks of a challenging foe.

Intemperance sprang from, or at least has followed closely in the wake of the Christian civilization of this advanced age. This being true, the question of the hour is: Will or will not the Christian civilization of this century confront this collosal evil and destroy it? This must be done, or intemperance—developing in hideous proportions—will eventually gain the supremacy of power and influence, and rule this Nation and the world with a corrupting, destructive and debauching hand.

It is not a sham battle in which the great moral forces of this Nation of people are arrayed in rank and file. The conflict is actual and real, and danger is to be apprehended. The liquor traffic is fraught with harm and danger. And if it is not suppressed, it bids fair to rise to the supremacy of power in this country, and rule this Nation, and in ruling it debauch it. And to-day—at this present crisis hour—it would tax the moral strength of this Nation to banish the sale and use of distilled liquor in the United States by Legislation. Inference can be drawn from what has been said, that the people of this country have the moral courage, and the moral strength to grapple with and destroy the blighting evil of intemperance. Again I revert to the fact, that drunkenness has become most prevalent and contagious and frightful in its results, in America at a time or period, when we are most amply prepared and qualified to resist its encroachment, and stay its ravages by the strong arm of the law.

It takes the moral element of strength to withstand the ravages of drunkenness, to turn back the tide of intemperance, and to resist the onward march of this destroying foe, and with moral strength—whatever else may be said for or against it—this Nation is grandly equipped. The temperance people of this country are not too feeble or effeminate to grapple with and destroy this enemy of the race which for a century in America has boldly challenged a mortal contest. The name is legion of those who challenge the existence of this infernal traffic, and debauching evil, of rum selling and rum drinking. And I cannot refrain from expressing my disapproval of, and hostility to any attempt of fanatical men to spring upon the people of this country a distinctive prohibition party, or political organization. The monstrous folly of such a scheme brands it as the work of unballanced enthusiasts. The weakness of such an enterprise borders upon imbecility. We have a political party that unites with other virtues—temperance, and champions temperance principles. The Republican party—the hero of a thousand conflicts—the party that bears upon its brow more laurels of triumph, in moral and political reform than was ever bestowed upon any political organization that has existed—is moving on to accomplish this grand and crowning reform of legislative prohibition. There is but one prohibition party in this country; that party is the Republican party. The great rank and file of that party are Christian temperance men.

The Republican party is the great prohibition party of America; and will without a blush or tinge of shame bear the standard of temperance in every State in the Union, when the proper time and opportunity presents itself. And I cannot but look with a feeling of mingled contempt and commisseration upon the efforts of overzealous men to spring upon the people a third party waving with frantic gusto a prohibition banner. Such efforts cannot but result each time in humiliating defeat, and bring odium upon the temperance cause. And every time and whenever the folly is repeated of crowding a distinctive prohibition party to the front, it but creates the impression in the minds of the people that the friends of temperance comprise but a body guard of soldiers, leading a forlorn hope, or facing certain defeat and disaster. It is enough to say that the efforts of such men and such parties signally fail. They have never approximated the accomplishment of what they have planned to do. And their prospects of success are diminishing rather than increasing in the sweep of time. It is clearly apparent that no respectable or intelligent purpose can be served by crowding the prohibition party upon the same field now occupied by the time honored and laurel wreathed Republican organization. I am in favor of the destruction of the liquor traffic. If the Republican party as a political organization having the power to do this, should refuse; I would desert its ranks, and would vote with the political party which if vested with the power would enact legislative measures favoring prohibition. For I look with devout horror upon any political party which in this Christian land unblushingly stands for the defense and protection of the damning liquor traffic which is debauching this Nation.

The fate of prohibition as a political issue is inseperably and indissolubly linked with the destiny of the Republican party. The temperance question stands related to the Republican party as the Bible stands related to Christian civilization. Defeat or destroy that political party and you eclipse in gloom, every ray of hope of ending the destructive rule and reign of rum. Men say the Republican party has fulfilled its mission. Such utterances to my mind are the veriest drivel. They are vagaries of a distempered head and heart. When the time comes for accomplishing results, this party will take the field in the campaign of temperance reform, and will win victories more decisive and brilliant than was ever won by glittering armies marching under waving banners. If, prohibition is ever declared throughout the States of the Union as it has been declared in Kansas and Iowa, the grand result will be accomplished by the Republican party, and not by a corporal guard band of enthusiasts sailing the dashing sea of moral reform under the head of "Prohibition."

I respect profoundly every man that is agitating this question of prohibition, whoever he may be. But to me there is something peculiarly ungrateful and abhorent in the action of men who are laboring for the accomplishment of this great end, to turn in hostility upon the great Party of moral reforms, which stands ready and fully equipped for this humane and patriotic work. And, viewed in the most charitable light, a third party, or prohibition party, in our national politics is a mere formal burlesque party. There is no precedent in the political history of either the Republics or Empires of the world showing that a third party was ever successful in accomplishing what it undertook.

I leave this phase of the subject for the discussion of one of greater importance. In the discussion of the great problem of temperance we have two civilizations with which to deal—a Christian civilization and a Paganistic civilization. The Christian civilization springs from the teachings of Christ. It draws its life and inspiration from the Word of Divine Truth, and is permeated with the Spirit of the true and living God. The Paganistic civilization, while it may not altogether deny the truthfulness of these Christianizing elements or principles, it is out of harmony with the religion of Christ, and out of sympathy with the great principles of moral reform, which the religion of Divine Revelation proposes to accomplish, and silently traverses and contraverses the eternal principles of right, of justice, and truth, which Christianity proposes to establish and perpetuate. You may be startled by the declaration that there is a Paganistic civilization in this Christian land. But the truthfulness of this declaration is overwhelming, and needs but to be pointed out.

Allow me this distinction. A man my be Paganistic in his views, and yet not be a Pagan. A man may be Paganistic in his views and principles, and yet not worship false gods. Again, a man who is out of sympathy and harmony with the religion of Christ, and with the spirit of the religion of revelation, is paganistic in his views. Or, in other words, if perchance we may simplify this truth, take Christ out of the universe, and all civilization is paganistic. Christian civilization had its origin in Christ. Before His advent

Pagan civilization swayed the sceptre of power over the world. That power has been broken, but Pagan civilization has its realm and domain to-day. Pagan civilization existed before Christ, and exists to-day wherever the conquest of the religion of Christ has not been made. Every civilization that leaves Christ out, and is out of sympathy with His kingdom of love and grace, and out of harmony with the truths of revelation, is paganistic in its origin and tendency.

All that is outside of Christ's kingdom is paganistic. Christian civilization had its origin in God. Pagan civilization had its origin in the worship of false gods, and denies the existence of the true and living God. It is the breath of that spirit that says there is no God. Christian civilization characterizes Christ as God himself. The chief distinction of paganism is that it denies Christ and rules him out of the universe. Therefore nations or individuals are paganistic who hold this view and cherish this spirit. A man living in this Christian land, whose hills and valleys are dotted with churches and sanctuaries for the worshiping of the living God, and is out of sympathy with Christ and the progress of His Kingdom of love and grace, is paganistic in his belief and views. The man who would smite down the religion of revelation and trample beneath his feet the holy Sabbath, consecrated to the worship of God, is paganistic in thought and action. If he worships false gods, he is a pagan. If he is hostile to the Kingdom of Christ, he is paganistic.

And in the political, religious or social affairs of this great Nation, the man who plants his feet upon principles that are not Christ like, is planting his feet upon paganistic principles, and will live to see those principles wither and perish, and then strewn as leaves by the breath of winter's desolation. This Christ principal, this Christian civilization of this century, is the stone which the Prophet, Daniel saw in his dream which was cut out of the mountain without hands and rolled down into the valley and which consumed all the kingdoms of the earth. And the Kingdom of Christ is to be established in their stead and is to be an universal Kingdom. That Kingdom is being established now. Notably in our own land. And I repeat what I have said before, that all that lies outside of this Kingdom of Christ is Paganistic. Generation after generation may perish from off the face of the earth but this Kingdom of Christ stands in its signal grandeur, proposing the evangelization and Christianization of the whole world. It is standing securely upon this abiding and eternal principle, that gives us faith and courage in the belief that intemperance and every form of evil will be crushed and ground to dust. And it is from this point of view that we are warranted in saying that the spirit and breath of hostility to the progress and conquest of the Kingdom of Christ, belongs not to the Christian civilization of this age, but rather to a Pagan civilization, that sprang up in an age of gloom and darkness.

Whatever is christian, whatever is Christ-like, whatever is associated with the religion of Christ, enlists the sympathies and draws support from the best element of society in this country. The banner of Christ and not the stars and stripes is in reality the ensign of this Nation. The Church of the living God is the greatest bulwark of strength in America, and this strength is being greatly augmented each year. Think you then that whatever it sets its hands to do it will fail to accomplish. And think you that in a protracted national contest that the christian people of this country will not be victorious. The universally prevailing sentiment of the Christian people of this country is that the sale of alcoholic beverages shall be prohibited by a national legislative law. They demand this in the name of Christ, in the name of the christian religion, in the name of christian civilization. Think you not that in the near future this demand will be granted and that christian America will, for once, stand before the Nations of the world freed from the bestial rum traffic and the ravages of strong drink.

Upon the broad shoulders of the Church rests the responsibility of this issue, upon it depends the victory. I wonder if there is a true christian man in America, that is not on the side of temperance and in favor of prohibition. In reality—I do not wonder about anything of the kind—if a man is a true christian and has the spirit of Christ, he can not be other than a temperance man and in favor of prohibatory measures. He cannot but be impressed with the words of the sacred writer, "no drunkard can enter the kingdom of heaven." And he knows by moral perception that a man may be a drunkard in principle and not in deed; he knows by moral intuition that a man who drinks that which produces drunkenness has the passions, the appetite, yea the heart and the principles of a drunkard. The act or custom of drinking no less than the actual evidences of drunkenness, impeaches and invalidates the professions of a man who claims to be a christian. In this great city the evidence that a minister habitually frequents bar-rooms, would be as fatal a charge as the actual evidences of drunkenness.

Then is it true that every Christian man in American is upon the side of temperance and temperance law? Yes, this is true. But there is one modification to be made. And this is a point I touch tenderly, and without one thought of malice. The Democratic party, that political organization now venerable and hoary headed with age, has unblushingly and without a tinge of shame boldly declared against prohibition, and has branded the measure as fanatical, inconsistent and irrational. The Church South in its political sympathies and affinities is allied to that party, and because the temperance question has a political bearing, the Southern Church remains silent and passes the issue by, unheeded and unnoticed. It is not revealing a new secret to say that the Democratic party has a strong affinity for the liquor traffic, and publicly and unblushingly declares against prohibition. As a consequence its votaries, whether Christian men. or otherwise, must in assent bow their heads and remain mute and noncommittal. Thereby the temperance cause is deprived of the aggressive and active support and co-operation of a large proportion of the Christian people of this country.

I do not mean to say that the constituency—the Ministers and Laymen of the Southern Church—are not men of temperance sentiments and temperance principles, as well as the constituency of the Northern Church; but I mean to say that they find themselves allied and united by chains that have grown so strong that they cannot well be broken, to a political party that boldly champions this dire evil and blighting curse of the liquor traffic; and which with brazen nonchalance says no law shall be enacted by this State or Nation depriving man of whisky, rum and brandy to his fill. I have but a questisn to ask. It is this; Christian men of Southern sentiment, of Southern principles, of Southern political faith—when the whisky traffic becomes a national issue, and the brave and noble men of this country convene at the ballot-box to settle irrevocably this question upon which the fate and destiny of political parties hinge—upon which side will you cast your vote? Will you, when such a crisis comes—and as sure as God reigns, it is swiftly coming—sacrifice your political faith and prejudices for the sake of your temperance and Christian sentiments and principles? This will be a crucial test for the Christian men throughout the South, who have for half a century loved, cherished and, we might almost say, worshipped at the shrine of the Democratic party.

That great human wrong—slavery—bred political differences between the North and South, that have not yet disappeared. And will scarcely disappear with the generation that now people this continent. Would to God we could heal them, or destroy them and even destroy their memory. Would to God, if it would avail for this purpose, we could destroy both the Republican and Democratic parties, and have their names and their deeds perish forever from our memory, and then begin afresh and anew religiously and politically. I for one would rather see such a violent destruction of all that goes to make up tne memory, the history and the existence of both these great National political parties, than to see the North and South of this land, which next to God, is the strongest object of affection in my heart—divided in sentiment, in impulse and in sympathy.

How unspeakably sad the history and memory of the rebellion. Slavery became a political issue, and rended this Nation with violence and destruction. Would that the great issue could have been settled at the ballot-box. But this was denied us. In its championship of the abolition of human slavery, the North believed it was right, and God crowned them with victory. The sad event has passed into history, and we but touch tenderly its mournful memory.

Whisky is fast becoming a political issue. The North, stands ready to-day to champion the suppression of the liquor traffic. But may God forbid that the North should be upon one side and the South upon the other side of this great National question. The North advocating its suppression; the South hesitating and objecting. But rather may they join hands and hearts as a Union of people, and as an United Nation. May God forbid that the political lines and boundaries should be drawn in this National contest over intemperance as it was drawn in the contest over slavery. But is this not the tendency. Is this not the outlook. Will this not be the inevitable result. I apprehend that every State in the North will declare prohibition, before a single State in the South makes a move or takes up the gauntlet. Watch the political events of this Nation for ten years and see. God grant that my pervisions may prove false. In discussing this question of prohibition as a National political issue and that is what it necessarily resolves itself into, I merely touch upon these points I have mentioned as points of interest and significance.

Whoever aids, or whoever opposes, whoever prays for its success, or whoever frowns upon the efforts, whatever men may think or say or do in favor of or in opposition to, one thing is clothed with the robe of certainty and armed with the weapon of assurance, and that is the triumph of prohibition, resplendent, universal and illustrious; and in the accomplishment of this grand and noble work we should know no North or South or East or West, but should unite our efforts as one Nation, that the example of this achievement might be beautiful and impress itself more deeply upon the current of the affairs of earth. This Nation of people will not rest or cease an active aggressive struggle until prohibition is an accomplished fact. The necessity of such a measure forces itself upon the heart, the conscience and the intellect of the christian people of this country. It is a triumph God sanctions and the world covets, and when accomplished how grateful will be the tidings of the victory to the hearts of the people of this country, this rum ridden, this rum cursed Nation. May God speed the day of triumph, but may the triumph not come until by your efforts we have earned it.

And in closing, permit me to say that whoever does not believe that in the fulness of time the liquor traffic will be removed, will be "chained," as it were, and "cast into the bottomless pit," has lived this life to a poor purpose, and is not *en report* with the designs, the purposes and the spirit of Christianity and Christian civilization. Christian civilization has this purpose in view, and to say that it will fail in accomplishing this purpose, is to say that Christian civilization will fail. Many of the wiseacres of this Nation, who stand well for intelligence and judgment, have put on record their opinion and belief that prohibitory measures are necessarilly a failure, and will prove disastrous to the interest of the the country. I will leave it to you if such opinions and views are not foreign to the spirit of Christianity.

The man who who surveys the frightful devastation, wreck and ruin caused by drunkenness upon either bank of the stream; throughout the world, eight hundred thousand lives annually sacrificed to appease the hunger of this dragon of destruction; almost that number of women widowed; three times that number of children made orphans; the world filled with crime, poverty and sorrow. Add to this record one million of men and women continually incarcerated within prison walls; and even all this is but a partial list belonging to the black category;—I say, the man who surveys all of this, and then says it is just and right that this thing should be; or whether just and right or not, it is to be perpetuated throughout the ages, protected and defended by law, is paganistic and not Christian in his views. And to my mind there is something revolting and frightful in the contemplation of the thought, that in this land of freedom, of enlightenment and religious culture any individual or class of men, or any political party should cast its fortunes with the rum selling and rum drinking element of society, champion their interests and seek to perpetuate this damning traffic of blight, of pestilence and of death.

When the yellow fever, cholera or any epidemic scourge sweeps over the country, the heads of the Government direct their attention to it, and the science and skill of the medical profession, throughout the land is brought to bear upon it, Cities are all quarantined, transportation suspended, and every remedy applied and precaution taken to prevent its spread and to eradicate and destroy every germ of the disease that exists. An argument from any source that such action and such a course was unwarranted or unnecessary, that the destroying contagious scourge should be protected and perpetuated, rather than destroyed, is in conscience and in reason, as valid and as rational an argument, as the one that the life destroying liquor curse should be protected by law, perpetuated and permanently associated with the civilization of this country, and sacredly bequeathed as a precious legacy to the children of the rising generation.

One of these arguments morally is as good and as valid as the other. Neither one of them is good for anything. The only argument I know of that is valid and that is gaining strength is that the accursed liquor traffic like some of the tyrannous or despotic kings of whom we have read, has had its reign of debauchery and destruction, and not only must, but shall be prohibited by law. And this is what is being borne hither, for this Nation, upon the swift wings of time. The very atmosphere we breath is filled with this sentiment. Twenty-five years more will witness the triumph of the Kingdom of Christ in the evangelization of Germany, Great Britain and America, three of the grandest Nations of earth. Coupled with that sacred conquest, we shall also witness the triumph of this great moral reform for which we are laboring and which is so dear to our hearts. The full orbed sun of the nineteenth century, will set in a serene sky, casting its golden rays, like a halo of glory over this land freed from the curse of strong drink, and the blight of intemperance.

Temperance in its Relation to Christian Civilization.

SHALL speak briefly upon temperance in its relation to Christian civiliza tion. While it is clearly evident that intemperance is a destroying evil, intimately associated with modern civilization, I shall endeavor to give plausible reasons for believing that Christian civilization will be able to event-ually crush and to destroy this evil. The sweep of centuries bring with them marked and important changes in the condition of the race. During the progress of the present century, we are witnessing the reign of melodrama and of sensationalism. We are living in an age of chivalry, of daring enterprise and lofty accomplishments. Animated and thrilled with the anticipation of results in the future that distance the past. The nations of earth are falling into rank, joining hands and moving with a quick step in the onward march of advancement, and we marvel at the grandeur and beauty of the achievements of modern times. We may signal out the sublime in history, but it does not afford a parallel to the splendid achievement of this day of civil liberty and Christian enlightenment.

The future of the race upon earth is bright with promise and radiant with hope to those who can discern or measure the influences that are at work, and that are to temper an control the passions, conduct and ambitions of men in the swift approaching age that border the millennial reign. To those who have faith in the triumph of moral ideas, of moral principles, of right over wrong, the future glows with promise, and the day-spring and dawn of ad-vancement lightens up the darkened pathway of life toward the goal of a perfect day—a day of loftier, holier, purer sentiment, conduct and living than the race hitherto has ever known.

It is true at present that there are rumors of discord and division, civil strife, clashings of factions, and rumors of national conflicts abroad, that perplex men's minds and fills their souls with fear, but these are, it may be, only dis-cordant passages in the grand symphony of human events, and these jarring notes that peal forth upon our ears and hearts will yet ultimate in perfect harmony. Strife will yet yield to peace, and the loftiest ambitions of men to promote, truth, honor, humanity and religion, will be crowned with triumph, and the brow of every patriot and philanthropist wreathed with a chaplet of immortelles. It must be so. Truth cannot perish. Right cannot fail. Justice will endure forever. Principles are eternal. Empires, Republics and Nations may wane and perish in their grandeur; but these essential principles of human government will abide forever.

Whoever does not believe in the complete triumph of the right and the overthrow of the wrong; the ultimate victory of the eternal principles of human justice, and the decline and final defeat of the wrong, of injustice, of viciousness and criminality; whoever does not believe in these things is walking in darkness, the mist of infidelity veiling his face and intercepting his vision. In the long run the right is destined to triumph; and in the long run whatever triumphs is right. A man who does not believe this, does not believe in God. He is standing upon Atheistic grounds. Victory, when the battle is fairly fought, settles the issues of right and wrong involved. The man who fights for a principle and wins in the conflict holds in his hands the credentials to the righteousness of the cause which he challenged. This is true of National affairs; and it is true of moral conflicts that are to determine the principles and laws by which social order is to be maintained, and human government perpetuated. And in the moral realm and sphere, that which is wrong, vicious, and destructive and debasing must be combatted and opposed as an enemy until it yields. And that is just what the best element of society is faithfully engaged in doing.

The coming ages slope toward grandeur and toward a royal termination of life upon earth with the race of mankind. We are living in an age of transition, from darkness to light, from bad to good, and the past does not mirror the future. It is not difficult to span the golden age with the bow of promise and of hope. Life upon earth with the race is yet to culminate in grandeur. Toward the lofty standard of divine truth and moral excellence, humanity is advancing, however slow the progress, and with whatever breaks between; and we watch and wait and labor, woed by the dawn of advancement for better things to come, expectantly and confidently looking for the ultimate victory of those cherished principles, truths and interests which we have championed.

In the struggle over these issues the race is not without encouragement. The twilight rays of a better day is breaking upon the world. More progress has been made within the last century than has been made before during all the preceeding ages of earth's history. Each succeeding year indicates an advancement, and with the ratio of increase increasing each year beyond computation, where is this progress to stop, if it is not to reach perfection? It is important to consider these questions and issues, touching the views and opinions of men upon the aims, purposes, accomplishments and possibilities of mankind in the struggle to free itself from those influences and evils, that destroy man's happiness, hinders his progress and mars his destiny. It is important to consider these questions in discussing the great problem of intemperance.

Men before they engage in a lifetime struggle of fighting the wrong want to determine in their own heart and convictions whether it is worth while to wage such a warfare. And in the great contest where moral truth and principles of honor of justice and of humanity are involed, it is important, to an eminent degree to determine what are the prospects and possibilities of winning the triumph in such a contest.

If modern civilization, the enlightenment of the ninteenth century, is not calculated and destined to lift mankind to higher grounds and to a higher plane of moral excellence and moral living; then the destruction of the evil of intemperance, might as well be abandoned. If there is no faith to be put in the successful issue of the humanitarianizing influences that are at work for the elevation and redemption of fallen men, then individual efforts in this direction are misapplied and fruitless.

Important changes are being marked upon the dial of time. Evolution in this age is effecting an improvement in the condition of mankind, socially, morally, politically and intellectually, and in every other respect. The world is making some progress. We are by degrees learning how to live. The race is gradually, step by step, rising to a higher plane of life. This is an age of thought, of culture, yea of grandeur. It is by no means a misfortune to live in this day of advanced civilization and enlightenment. But how did we reach this lofty and desirable plane of life? The answer is not far to get. We reached it by evolution. Our people and our race sprang—so far as we know —not from the monkey tribe, but from paganism. At least, our ancestors once groped in the darkness of semi-civilization. But evolution has done wonders. It has made us a great Nation; and we are proud of our race and the enlightened civilization of the nineteenth century. Those accomplishments and achievements of to-day, that excite our admiration, dazzle and captivate our senses and bewilder our minds, are attributable to evolution along a moral and intellectual plane. All that we have and are, that is desirable or worth mentioning, those things of which we are proud, our government, its laws, its politics; our schools, our seminaries, our churches: our religion, social and intellectual culture; all these things that dignify and grace our people and our Nation, are the products of evolution, and do not date back to a very distant past; at least, not to antiquity.

The Bible and civilization have walked hand in hand and abreast in the march of progress, and in the sweep of ages as thoughts and opinions have been evolved, they have been crystalized into customs and laws. Thus have we achieved greatness as a Nation and crowded our pantheon with rich accessions of glory; thus have we risen from the mists of Pagan obscurity and darkness toward the light of civil liberty, intellectual culture and religious tolerence. We have stripped the manacles from our limbs disenthralled our minds; and to-day stand out under the blue and stars of· the firmament—the glittering banner of heaven, as freemen and noblemen. How have we accomplished such great things? How have we reached such peerless heigths? by evolution, by a gradual progressive development and unfolding toward this higher plane of life.

I would not for all the world of wealth be guilty of unassociating the Bible and the religion of divine revelation with the pure, lofty and ideal civilization and enlightenment of America, and of the nineteenth century in other lands than our own. The Bible largely has been our guide and has served as a precursor. It has been a lamp to our feet as we have trend the rugged path of scientific and intellectual progress. We could have done nothing without it. Without its gleam we walk in the night, until at length we reach the brink of life and then plunge over a precipice into the regions of everlasting darkness. In its light we walk a pavement of gold leading up from earth to heaven. There is not, there can be, no enlightenment where the Bible is not found, and where the religion of Christ has not made its conquests.

As the Constitution of our Government is the pillar of our national temple, so religion is the pillar in the intellectual temple, which the advanced nations of the world have builded, at whose shrine men worship. Take away religion and the stately temple would crumble to the earth in ruins. But better than this religion is the strength and support of individual Christian character. The Bible is the only foundation stone upon which we can with any degree of safety erect the fair structure of life. And upon individual effort and character depends the strength and perpetuity of our Nation. Men must confront the great problem of life individually; face its issues and fight its battles in the strength with which God has endowed them. "The fountains of our strength as a people and as a Nation, spring from individual life." Then how manifestly important that the lives of our people individually should be pure, that the strength of our Nation may be enduring? And how important that the aims and purposes of men individually should be pure, and that they should establish a lofty ideal of character, striving ever to attain unto perfection. It is such an ideal of character the Bible affords, to which Divine revelation points. Christ the Son of God was the perfect, the Archetypical man, and toward His Divine standard of moral excellence and purity of character mankind is making some progress.

Moral culture is the only abiding foundation for human character. It is the rock upon which we build, and upon which we stand. The Bible, the word of God, is our text book, and with it in hand, we can make some progress. Its silent influence nerves the race for noble attainments. In its light we move forward. The diversified inventions and improvements that characterize this advanced age are intimately associated with the progress of Christianity. Surely this generation has made marvelous progress. Developed and perfected giant schemes and enterprises. Its royal achievements eclipse the past, and interpenetrates the future with the rays of hope and promise. For we as a Nation are but crossing as it were the threshold of life in the accomplishments of great possibilities. We are standing as it were in the mists of the dawn or twilight of a brilliant day. In the radient future we behold a perfected government; a Republic clothed in white and crowned with roses.

This may have a tinge of the idealistic, but no thought can fathom or intellect conceive of the dazzling splendor of the achievements of the human race in the golden future in its career and life upon earth. Moral impulses and principles are yet to rule the world, and that with a grandeur that will cause us to tremble at their beauty and significance. No mind can conceive of the sublime feature to be revealed and perfected by an enlightened race, free to use to the best advantage every instrumentality placed within its reach.

Intellectual culture, religious truth and human government are in their infancy and will require centuries yet in which to develop and unfold, and no ideal that may be conceived will transcend the perfection, symmetry and beauty in human character that may be reached in the ages to come. A millennial day will yet dawn, and the centuries yet unborn will be lit with celestial rays gleaming from the throne of heaven.

But some one says there is a dark side to be mirrored in our minds, and the reflection it casts is darker than the night of doom. The ideal age of enlightment which you have pictured, those lofty attainments and accomplishments that are yet to be reached after the lapse of ages, are preeminently desirable, the very thought of them thrills and electrifies the mind. The glowing anticipation of such realizations quicken every emotion of heart and intellect. But civilization, in its purest and loftiest form, where it has made its most signal and brilliant conquests, is not unattended with crime and evils, that would put to shame the Pagan Nations of the distant orient climes. Come with me, you say, and we will journey to a Heathen land. We will mingle with the people of India and China, and learn from them a lesson in the art of simple civilization, freed well nigh from every taint of immorality.

Take, you say, China with her four hundred millions of inhabitants, and she is comparatively free from crime. Profanity, theft, dishonesty, drunkenness, debauchery and cruel murder are comparatively unknown among that antiquated race. Those things, you say, are most rank and rife among those Nations where your boasted civilization has attained nearest to perfection. There is a semblance of truth floating upon the surface of such an argument as this, but an analytical view of it discloses the deception underlying it. I do not propose to discuss the Chinese question, but shall speak a few moments upon China, in illustration of a truth I wish to emphasize. It is said that immorality and crime are comparatively unknown in China; that in America, with her fifty millions of people, there are ten murders committed to where there is one committed in China, where there is a population of four hundred millions, a proportion of one to eighty to an equal number of inhabitants of each respective Nation. We will concede that this is true; but while the Chinese are an innocent set of people, harmless and dove like, it has been discovered on the other hand that they never do any good. They are as worthless as they are innocent. They simply live, pass through this world and die, and it is not definitely known that they ever leave any footprints in the sands of time. At least generation after generation of them perish from off the earth without ever giving to humanity an impulse. They are, as it were, prisoners bound with the iron chains of ignorance, superstition and paganism. They are manacled and bound in chains of darkness and have no freedom of limbs with which to commit crimes. They do not intellectually and morally rise to the dignity of respectable criminals, at least such criminals as America produces. They are slaves to their own heathenish customs; prisoners within the walls of Pagan institutions, and it is not to be wondered at that they are innocent of the commission of crimes.

Take a man, a criminal, if you please, and build a great stone wall around him, and you have no idea of how innocent he will be while kept within that inclosure. There is nothing within the walls for him to steal. He couldn't commit crime if he wanted to. But how worthless he would be, while thus imprisoned within huge stone walls! Over in Jeffersonville there are five hundred hardened criminals confined in one prison. They are innocent, innoffensive men while thus behind prison bars. There is no possibility of their committing crimes, while fettered and guarded, and enslaved. But give them their freedom and see what will happen. Those who are criminals at heart will indulge in crime again. Now, civilization, at least Christian civilization, liberates men; giving them their freedom. It strips their limbs of manacles and turns them out in the world as freemen. It may be fraught with danger; for it gives to men who have criminal dispositions and hearts the liberty to commit crime. But it is the best thing that can be done for men. Give men their liberty, to do as they please, and then appeal to their hearts and consciences to influence them to do what is right and refrain from the wrong and from the perpetration of crime. It is better for them than the prison pen and the galling chains of tyranny clanking about their limbs. This is the way to develop and perfect a noble manhood.

In the transition from a lower state of civilization to a higher state, the race must pass through a period or era of crime. This is inevitable. It comes in the very nature and course of things. Crimes or criminal indulgences are necessary accompaniments and characteristics of modern progressive civilization. It is to be lamented. But the struggle toward loftier attainments and nobler accomplishments, is not to be abandoned, because as we progress crime increases and becomes fearfully prevalent. It is clearly apparent that it is through such a thrilling and eventful period or era, of crime and vicious indulgence our people are passing at the present time, in the transition from a lower grade to a higher plane of moral excellence and nobler manhood. And if China, and I speak of this nation only as a representative Pagan Nation, ever travels this royal way toward a higher civilization and enlightenment, they will necessarilly and essentially experience what we are experiencing. China, and all other pagan nations, are living away down on the lowest plane of intellectual and moral life. China, in fact, is so low down that she is beneath our feet. Those nations are not turning out illustrious criminals or anything else worthy of note. They are inert, worthless, trifling, and the world is in no way benefitted by their living in it. The same cannot be said about America and Great Britain, notwithstanding their damning record of crime and illustrious criminals.

Think, if you please, of China with her four hundred millions of inhabitants, with a territory almost as large as our own Nation, boasting indefinite antiquity, with, at last reports, thirteen miles of telegraphy and a few hundred miles of railroad. Place by her side India with her hundreds of millions of inhabitants, with a history as old as the history of the world. Yet, neither of these nations have ever furnished to humanity and modern civilization one single idea or one impulse. You could sweep the inhabitants of each of these nations, together with a score of others similar to them from off the face of the earth, and religion would not lose an impulse. The social, political, and intellectual progress of the enlightened nations of the earth would not feel the effect.

A few years ago, a destructive cyclone swept three hundred thousand of the population of China into the sea, and not a ripple of the wave of excitement ever reached the shores of our continent.

But now to the issue and practical lesson of the hour. Our modern civilization, however lofty its ideal, however pure its motives, is trammelled in its progress, beset and environed with crime and criminal practices and vices. Men with viciated tastes and depraved hearts spring up in our midst and take advantage of the liberty which the laws and sanctions of our free government gives them, and by their lawlessness, bring reproach upon our people and our Nation. The abuse of the liberty, which society and our laws give men often shock the sensibilities of those upon whom the burden of civil government rests. These abuses are often carried to extremes. Lawlessness sometimes becomes rampant, riots break out, mob violence sweep the land, and a reign of terror threatens the people. Men abound who have propensities for gambling, and who do not blush to engage in illicit enterprises, burglarize, rob, and even murder their fellow man for his paltry gold. And sometimes when we view the prevalency and viciousness of crime in its worst form, and reflect upon the helplessness of the law to restrain the evil passions and propensities of men, we are tempted to ask ourselves the question, and then answer it in the affirmative: Is not, after all, our boasted civilization of the Nineteenth Century a failure? I doubt not but that many asked themselves the question last *summer when our beloved President Garfield was shot down in the path of duty by a fiendish demoniac, is not our civil law, our boasted institutions of free government a failure? And as during the slowly waning days of the weary summer he laid upon his couch of pain, of suffering and of death, what must have been his silent thoughts as he reflected upon our government, clothed as it is in pearless, grandeur, dignity and majesty, the government he had loved and cherished better than his own life, to whose interests he had consecrated his noble life; yet after all proving incapable of affording him, its chief magistrate, protection from a violent death at the hands of one of his subjects.

But we cannot dwell longer upon generalities, but concede at once that malignant and distressing abuses, mar the symmetry, beauty and grandeur of our free government and progressive civilization.

From the attack springs the defense. For every abuse there is a remedy. Against the myriad forms of abuse and licensed crime that have attacked our cherished liberty, and carried distress, suffering and sorrow to the hearts and homes of our people, there has been an organized defense and opposition waged. And humanity, sheltered beneath the wide extended wings, and guarded by the loving surveillance of an enlightened Christian civilization, is not going to suffer forever in our own beloved country. Crusades against the wrong, against vice, against those organized means and influences that are calculated to burden and distress humanity, and to rob the people of those fruition and blessings which civilization is intended to bestow, have been made with signal results. Systematized organization for the defense and protection of truth, of honor, of virtue, of humanity, and for the alleviation of suffering and harm, inflicted by the reign of abuse and lawlessness, have done effectual work throughout our own land.

It was for this purpose, for the accomplishment of this lofty and noble work, that this*"Temple of Honor" was organized, and stands to-day clothed with the dignity, title and authority of a humanitarian institution, moving forward in its sphere of action, fulfilling a divine mission, accomplishing a sacred work; individuals united in fraternal fellowship, joined hand and heart in fidelity in the consecrated work and labor of love.

The supreme abuse with which we have to contend and which has swept in violent destruction across our land as the terrific cyclone sweeps in releutless fury across the green fields in mid summer has been, and is now intemperance. That demon, strong drink, has been the most malignant assailant and hostile foe, to human happiness, to moral culture and to the advance of civilization in our own land and throughout the Nations of the world, with which mankind has had to contend. Intemperance in its most malignant form, existing as it does in fearful prevalency, is calculated to mar, to blight and utterly destroy social happiness, and wreck and desolate the homes whose sanctity it invades, and the feeble resistance of a loving hand cannot stay its ruthless steps and desecrating influence when it has once crossed the threshold of the social circle and the domestic household.

Intemperance, the monstrous evil of the age, stalk about and among us, and its step, like the leviathan's tread, shakes the earth. Its deadly influence is felt to the remote corners of the earth. But its greatest ruin, devastation, and desolation is wrought in the very heart and center of the most enlightened nations of the earth. Our own beloved land of freedom has become the asylum of the drunkard, and our Government has thrown her arms of protection around the distiller, the drunkard maker. We are one and all familliar with the fateful ravages, ruin and sorrow wrought by this pestilential evil and deadly curse. And the better thinking and better principled class of men and women throughout the world, in all lands have organized and planned an opposition to the cruel work of this hideous foe to human happiness and human liberty. The faithful few who form the nucleus of every humane organization and institution, are lifting hand and voice, and putting heart and will in this Divine work of staying the tide of intemperance. Some progress is being made. A myriad influences are at work, and there can be but one result. Intemperance the hideous visaged demon of ruin, of pestilence and of death, will eventuallly be crushed and charred beneath the burning chariot wheels of a righteous public sentiment. And our Nation will be a free Nation. And no man among us will wear upon his brow the darkling-brand and curse of a drunkard.

We will reach this high and noble plane of moral life eventually ; when religion, when truth and rightousness shall have made their conquests; when the right, the good, the pure shall have been vindicated ; when the false, the wrong, the viscious shall have been relegated to the realms of darkness ; then shall our Christian civilization shine forth with the lustrious glory of the Son of Righteousness, and all the world shall behold its glory.

Delivered before the Temple of Honor, July, 1882.

We need not deceive ourselves with the thought that we will be able to effect a speedy overthrow of the deeprooted evil and curse of drunkenness, of intemperance and of the sale of strong drink in our midst. Our efforts should be, and will be, incessant and unrelenting, and the influence of our efforts, mingled with the influence of others will be felt when the crises comes, when intemperance will be stormed as an enemies fortress, when the enemy and their cause shall perish together in common ruins. If we love the cause of temperance we must be willing to show our fidelity by working without being able to see any visible results. Intemperance cannot be suppressed through the influence of temperance organization and associations alone. It will require the concurrent influence of every humane, benevolent and religious institutions upon the face of the earth to cope with and to overcome this giant towering monstrous curse of intemperance.

A great many people are confidently depending upon legislation to banish the inhuman traffic of liquor; but this will not prove effectual. I have no desire to discourage any one who is sanguinly relying upon this means to effect the reformation of the world, and to reclaim mankind from the blighting curse of intemperance. But I conscientiously apprehend that legislation will not prove equal to the task. We with one accord say that licensing the rumseller, putting the badge of loyalty upon him, and propecting him by the majesty of the law in his infamous enterprise of selling liquor, wrecking homes and destroying human life, we say that this is a reflection upon the Statesmanship of our Nation. It does seem so, but for awhile, at least, we have got to endure this state of affairs. This thing of licensing the manufacture and traffic of strong drink, then shuddering, groaning and weeping over the sad and deplorable results is an unanswerable commentary upon the Statesmanship of our times, even in our land of progress and intelligence; but we are far off from the day of perfection, and for awhile this thing must be endured. Some of our Statesmen are drunkards, and perhaps but few, if any of them are boldly in favor of legislation against the liquor traffic.

A great work remains to be accomplished, the suppression of intemperance by legislation cannot be effected until christian civilization shall have reached a higher plane, and men's beliefs and principles shall have been improved, and they shall have been lifted to a higher plane and higher grounds of intellectual and moral life; and when this is accomplished intemperance, without the interference of legislation, will disappear. An enlightened christian public sentiment will dissipate the evil of itself.

But some one says we are depending upon local option, and have built our hopes upon it in accomplishing prohibition; but you are unable through legislation to accomplish what you have undertaken yet for awhile. You have been working with local option for ten or fifteen years, and your progress has been very slow. You have carried your point in two or three States, but there is a degree of doubt lingering about the results in relation to them; and by a generous estimate it will take you twenty-five years longer to work public sentiment up to that point where, through legislation, you will be able to banish the liquor traffic from every State in the Union. And if you are not careful the progressive sweep of an enlightened Christian sentiment will accomplish the result of destroying intemperance before legislation can be effectually brought into operation.

But you say that that is highly idealistic, to say that in twenty-five years the race will have so improved in morals, and will have such correct ideas of respectability, of right, of honor, and that men will have such a high regard for themselves that they will not be guilty of compromising their integrity, their principles, and their lofty views of a noble manhood, by indulging in the vicious and criminal custom of social drinking. It is true that this is looking forward to an ideal civilization. But even so, we must approach very much nearer a state of idealistic civilization than we have reached at present before we can even suppress intemperance by legislation, or by any other possible means we can comprehend or conceive of. It is true, if we were flush with Christian Statesmen, they might take hold of this mooted problem of intemperance and settled it by legislation against the sale of strong drink. But we haven't got these Christian Statesmen, and consequently we must wait until we can raise them, or reform the morals and principles of those we have. Meantime a Christian public sentiment will be making rapid strides toward the solution of the same problem. For while you are teaching Statesmen temperance principles and habits, you can set to work and reform the whole enlightened world.

Legislation against the liquor traffic would be very desirable; but legislalation under our form of government must be sustained and backed by public sentiment and public opinion. At the present time we have not got Statesmen who are disposed to legislate against the liquor trade, and had we such Statesmen, we have not, at least in a great many States, a public sentiment to sustain them in such a measure. But I have faith to believe that the evolution of the age will in our own land produce men with brains and heart disposed to lay hold of this blighting curse of intemperance, and in righteous indignation destroy it, even though this age should fail to produce men competent the task. I do not believe that intemperance as it stalks about to-day carrying untold and unnamable sorrow and suffering to the hearts and homes of millions of people, will exist in America in the full blaze of the twentieth century.

But oh, what woes and pangs of sorrow and suffering may have to be endured by humanity before that day of deliverance. But there is no help for this, for the moral state or condition of society and of humanity at large to-day would absolutely not admit of or sustain total abstinence. Men are working with might and main to accomplish that which is a practical impossibility. Educate, Christianize the world. Bring humanity, far and near, to Christ. This will solve the temperance problem. But you say that is not practical. It is quicker and easier to legislate against the sale and use of liquor than it is to Christianize the world. But I answer you cannot do either upon the impulse of the moment. The attempt to do either is a herculian task, and overtaxes the strength and energies of the men of this generation.

And now finally, for the individual drunkard, who is on the highway in his course of ruin and of death, I commend Christ the Savior of mankind rather than the temperance pledge. A temperance pledge may serve some purpose before a man becomes a drunkard, but after he becomes a drunkard it requires something better. Christ taken into the heart as a Savior, I believe is the only influence upon earth or in the skies that has the power to rescue and save the drunkard, and lift him from the defilements of hell to the purity of heaven.

When Christ,, during his public life and ministry, went about casting out. devils; and the poor victims of the demons cried in anguish and fell upon the stones and cut themselves, the people marveled at his miraculous power. So some people may affect to be astonished when men appeal to Christ to cast out the demon of intemperance; but I am convinced that Christ alone has the power to do his.

Let us, dear friends, fight on, work on, in this temperance cause. Let us not be discouraged, for we shall reap a golden harvest of reward if we faint not. Let us work as if working not alone for humanity, but for the Divine Master, trusting God for the victory, looking to Heaven for our reward.

Intemperance in our own land is committing fearful ravages. Its tidal wave sweeps in resistless power over the country. We cannot at present stay that tide. The best we can do is to erect barriers around our homes and loved ones, and now and then rescue and save some poor victim perishing in the tide. And those who succeed this generation, as they also fight in the temperance cause will be grateful to us for the battles we have fought and the victories we have won. And after awhile, as ages pass by, an illustrious victory will be won in this campaign, and intemperance will perish forever amid the flame and din of battle. And in all our land, our beautiful land, from the Atlantic coast to the golden strands of the Pacific, from the Northern Lakes to the Sunny Gulf, wherever freedom finds a home, wherever the beautiful starry ensign of our Nation floats, there shall not be a drunkard found.

Strong Drink Degrading and Ruinous.

TRONG drink degrading and ruinious in its tendency and results, is the proposition affirmed. It is probably worth our while to devote an hour to the discussion of this painfully interesting subject. This phase, more perhaps than any other of the temperance question, comes nearer home to us individually and personally. If strong drink is debauching the lives and morals of our people—especially our young men—we want to familliarize ourselves with this deplorable and unwelcome fact, that we may, if possible devise some practical remedy. Drink is a vortex of ruin. It is a Niagara over whose dashing precipice nearly one million of human beings annually plunge to ruin and to death, and the power of human will and human strength cannot stop this work of destruction. But strong drink does not alone destroy life, ending it prematurely and robbing man of his best and most fruitful years, but it destroys the harmony, grandeur and sacredness of life, and renders the life of its victim wretched, and a step beyond this, and this is the saddest of all, it murders the soul.

Ten thousand different forms of evidence can be adduced to prove the truthfulness of this declaration with which I have prefaced this address. So transparent and universally prevalent are the facts and evidences attesting the affirmed proposition that strong drink is morally, intellectually and physically degrading and debasing, and so familliar are you with the facts and arguments usually brought to bear upon this phase of the temperance question that at a glance it may seem unnecessary to consider it at length. But our minds may be renewed, our hearts quickened and our courage strengthened for the battle we have to fight by refreshing our memories with a review of this subject. Almost every citizen of our land has witnessed with their own eyes the fateful results springing from the use of strong drink. Go where you may, following the sun in its orbit around the earth and you will find evidences of the ruin and desolation wrought by the pestilential scourge of rum and alcoholic beverages. The distressing fact that the sale and use of rum, mars the grandeur, hinders the progress and blights the prospects of our cherished Christian Civilization, intrudes itself upon the mind of every thoughtful intelligent man. Blind indeed to every perception of moral truth must be the man who does not grasp, realize and understand this fact.

Intellect is going to rule the world. Intellectual supremacy will take the throne, and sway the sceptre of power and dominion over the world. The intellectual Christian men are struggling for the supremacy of influence and power in the control and management of human and civil government. And the prospects of this eternally sublime achievement brightens with the swift fleeting days of this closing century. It is the design of Christian philanthropy, it is the purpose of religion to lift mankind heavenward, toward a higher and nobler plane of moral and intellectual life, so that it may escape as far as possible some of the suffering, degradation, poverty and crime that now burden the race. If there is one thing more than another standing in the way of this sublime and humane achievement, it is the vitiating, destroying rum traffic. It is a solemn and serious consideration, that the rum traffic in our bright and prosperous land should destroy the lives of seventy thousand of our citizens, but the deplorable result does not stop there. Wherever you find intemperance you will find ignorance, indolence, squalid poverty, and frail, feeble-minded men and women and children. Where drunkenness prevails, men descend rather than ascend in the scale of morals and intellect.

It is the design of good men, of the better thinking and acting class of men, to remedy this evil, to amend this fault. The great moral element of society is at work with might and main to free mankind from the curse of drink and drunkenness. Lured by the star of hope, men are pressing on with united hands and hearts to accomplish this great purpose and end. The success of the undertaking depends upon the progress of Christian civilization, and the advance of moral and intellectual culture among the masses. But the suppression of the liquor traffic is not the subject for discussion at this time. The question to be asked and answered at this time is: What does strong drink do for men morally and physically? What is the effect upon the morals and life of men individually? I could occupy the time by expressing my own views and sentiments upon this subject, but instead of that, I shall endeavor to impress your minds by the use of excerpts from other writers and speakers; and shall bring the thoughts and views of some able men to bear upon this phase of the temperance problem. For there are very few men and women known to the world for their intellectual culture and attainments, but have put on record their views of this damning curse of strong drink.

Mr. Baird, of California, in a lecture upon the liquor traffic and its ruinous effects likens it to the City of Hell. He said by way of introduction, "It is impossible to appreciate the greatness of an army by seeing it in detail, a company here, a regiment there, and a battalion yonder. The same is true of the liquor traffic. We cannot judge it by seeing it in detail." The speaker then proceeded to take his audience to an imaginary height and show them this traffic concentrated. He first showed them a vast country devoted to the growing of grain and fruit which is rotted in the production of strong drink. He then pictured "The City of Hell" in the center of this vast country with its long streets lined with distilleries, breweries and grog-shops, a city which is emphatically a manufacturing city. He pictured the army of moderate drinkers, closely followed through the streets of the city by the army of confirmed drunkards; also the army of tramps made so by strong drink; the army of 75,000 fallen women, the legitimate outgrowth of the liquor traffic; and the army of 200,000 starving and almost naked children made so by the traffic. He described a Sunday morning with no church bell or churches, but with 10,000 beer gardens all in full blast; a court-house ten stories high, with 500 court rooms in which cases growing out of the liquor traffic are constantly being tried, a poor-house containing 150,000 inmates all of whom were comfortable and happy until strong drink had made them otherwise; an insane asylum with 80,000 insane and idiots, made so through this same traffic; a hospital with 160,000 sick and maimed, a penitentiary twenty stories high, near which were 200 raised platforms for the execution of rum criminals. He conducted his hearers through the valley of suicide; showed them a great cave two miles long where innumerable victims were suffering with delirium tremens, and took them down by the river of death where 60,000 of the victims of the cup die every year.

This picture, dark as it is, is not overdrawn. In reality it but faintly represents the terrible evil of intemperence. Think then what must be the true character of an enterprise about which such violent things can be said and yet not do it justice.

The New York Telegram in an editorial says: "The evils bred by liquor are so vast and terrible that it is no wonder that periodically an immense sense of the outrages to which it has given birth, seizes the more reputable part of the community. It is safe to say that the largest and better part of the population of New York City is sick to the soul with the crimes that have been perpetrated in the name of drink. All the sins and vices that beset human nature are locked up in that terrible liquor which sparkles so gladly, woes so irresistably, and is simply a liquid hypocrit, a beverage whose drops are burning snares."

A gentleman in New York City lecturing upon the rum traffic says: "If all the stores in which liquor is sold in New York City could be arranged in a line they would reach seventeen miles. The revenue derived from this traffic by the city and government is $300,000, while the criminals and paupers it throws upon the State costs the State $8,000,000. If that sum was devoted to some purpose that repaid us, if it brought us increased education or improvements of any kind we might tolerate it; but there is nothing we can derive from it. Our charitable and educational enterprises cost $1,500,000 while $70,000,000 goes to the liquor traffic, or an average of $70 apiece for every man, woman and child. Remember too, he says, how poverty and crime stalk about in this great city are directly traceable to intemperance. Learn the story of every poor beggar, man or woman or child that calls at your door for alms, and you will find that drunkenness underlies their misfortunes.

A writer treating of the relation of intemperance to crime, says: "Or if the victim of the traffic is naturally vicious, strong drink excites and fortifies the evil tendencies of his nature, and nerves him to deeds of darker guilt than he would otherwise perpetrate. The oft-quoted circumstance attending the killing of President Lincoln is a case in point. Brandy was the demon which nerved the courage and steadied the arm of the assassin ere the dastardly deed could be done.

At the trial of a criminal for a murder committed in the city of Cold-water, a few years ago, it was proved that the prisoner drank no less than thirteen times at a single bar in that city on the day of the murder, and before the crime was committed. The deed was pre-determined; but strong drink fortified the criminal purpose, and induced the necessary recklessness.

Idleness and poverty tend to produce crime, and strong drink is the cause of most of the indolence and pauperism from which the ranks of vice are recruited throughout the world."

Sir Matthew Hale, Lord Chief Justice of England, said nearly two hundred years ago: "Drink is the cause of four-fifths of all crimes;" and modern jurists have seen no reason for reviewing the judgment.

The Hon. John C. Park, district attorney for the county of Suffolk, Massachusetts, affirmed that careful observation during his incumbency in office led him to the conclusion that ninety-nine hundredths of all crime committed were the result of intemperance.

As a counter evidence that these declarations are true let us look for a moment at the decrease of crime where prohibition has been enforced. Lord Hamilton, a member of the British Parliment, testified that in the county which he represented—a county containing 10,000 inhabitants—where former-.y scenes of drunkenness, riot and strife were common, and where a large po-.ice force was necessary for the preservation of peace and the protection of life and property, subsequently, under prohibition, the district became so quite and orderly that not a policeman was required within its bounds, and at the same time the poor rates were reduced one-half. In the town of Low Moor, England, there is a population of 1,100, and not a dram shop in the place; there is no jail or lock-up, no constable or policeman. Order reigns supreme. In Potter County, Pensylvania, liquor bas been excluded under local option, and the jail is without an inmate one-half the time.—*H. M. Joy in Lever.*

In Soltaire, England, a town of 11,000 inhabitants, there is complete prohibition of all intoxicating liquors. Pauperism and crime are almost wholly unknown.

"In Bessbrook, Ireland, with four thousand people, the sale of liquor is completely prohibited. Result: No poor-house, pawnshop, or police station, and peace and industry reign supreme." "Vineland, N. J., with ten thousand inhabitants, has enjoyed for years the total prohibition of the liquor traffic. Three hundred dollars a year pays the cost of crime. Taxes only one per cent on valuation."

"Seven temperance towns in Delaware county, New York State, with a population of about fifteen thousand people, have averaged for the past eight years less than twelve dollars each for pauperism, crime, police justice and excise. While Coxsaxie, of N. Y., with a population of three thousand, submits to cost for crime, pauperism, etc., to the amount of $1,200."

"In 1880, the total number of persons arraigned in the police courts of rum-cursed New York City was 71,699, and of these, 50,000 were for intoxication and disorderly conduct; of the remaining 21,000 a very large proportion were for crimes growing out of the liquor curse."

Some newspaper, addressing itself to the public, says: "Nearly all the saloons of the country are owned and run by persons of foreign birth, who have very little sympathy with the prosperity of the Nation. These drinking places are the cesspools of vice and crime, a thousand times greater than the aggregate of their licenses and taxes paid."

A graphic writer tells the truth about the moral degradation of the rum traffic, in an article which he calls "Contrasts." He says: "Every rag stuck into a window to keep out the cold from a drunkard's home denotes a contribution towards buying new suits for the rum-seller and his family. The more elegance and ease in the rum-seller's family, the more poverty, degradation, and despair in the families of those who patronize him. The corner grogshop, with large plate-glass windows and marble floors, is paid for by the tenants of other landlords who refuse to let their buildings for such purposes. The more plate-glass and marble slabs there are in the rum-shop, the more soiled garments must be stuck in the windows of their patrons to keep out the cold air, the more silk flounces upon the dress of the rum-seller's wife, the cheaper the calico upon the wife and children of his patrons. The more spacious the parlor, and brighter the fire of the rumsellers. the more scantily furnished and colder the abodes of those who patronize him. While the rumseller drives his $1,000 span, his customers cannot even afford a five-cent horse-car. From the bung-hole of every barrel of liquid damnation that is sold by the dramsellers there flows a constant stream of drunkards, criminals, paupers, tramps, lunatics, and imbeciles, to fill poor-houses, houses of correction, jails and prisons. What blasted hopes, ruined homes, and paupers' graves are the relics of the trade! Every dollar that the owner of the rum-shop, and his rum-selling tenant put into their pockets, comes out of the pockets of the poor men, and is a dead loss, so far as the public good is concerned. Worse than that, the more rum sold, the more burdens there are imposed upon the honest citizens and taxpayers. The richer the landlord and his rum-selling tenants grow, the poorer becomes the landlord who lets his buildings for tenements and legitimate business. It is an undisputed fact that the laboring man who has a family cannot indulge liquor-drinking, and pay his landlord and grocer."

WHICH DOES IT DO?—If whisky has ever organized an institution whose aim was the upholding of Christ's kingdom, or has ever reformed a drunkard, or saved a lost or ruined soul, we have failed to see it. Does it add converts to the Church or converts to the penitentiary? Does it add philosophers and Statesmen to our Nation, or does it add subjects to our asylum, and paupers to the work-house? Does it educate the mind, or does it dethrone reason? Does it create love, peace and happiness or strife, quarreling, and misery?— *Meteor.*

"What is whisky bringing?" asked a dealer in that article, one day. He meant to ask how much it is selling for.

A gentlemen who heard the remark took it in an entirely different sense from that.

"What is whisky bringing?" do you ask. I'll tell you: "It is bringing men to prison and to the gallows, and it is bringing women and children to poverty and want."

There never was a truer answer than this.

It is estimated that it sends to prison every year one hundred thousand men and women.

Twenty thousand children are sent to the workhouse annually by drink.

Three hundred murders are caused by intemperance every year. Two hundred thousand children are made orphans every year, by this dreadful evil; and sixty-five thousand are killed by intemperance every year in this country.

Dr. J. G. Holland forcibly says: "I neither drink wine nor give it to my guests. Strong drink is the curse of the country and the age. Sixty thousand men in America every year lie down in the grave of the drunkard. Drink has murdered my best friends, and I hate it. It burdens me with taxes, and I denounce it as a nuisance, on which every honest man should put his heel. I do not ask you to put your heel on the drunkard, but to make the spirit of your guild so strict and pure that no man of your number will dare to trifle with your opinion and sentiments on the subject."

The Churchman says: "There is nothing in the world more inexcusable than the toleration of the rum-shop. They have not the least right to exist. They are conceived by a desire to get one's living for nothing beyond that of standing behind a counter, and begotten by a willingness to do any amount of harm to one's neighbor. Almost every occupation by which men get their living has the semblance of usefulness. But rum-selling has not the faintest claim to any such quality. The money that is spent in rum-shops had better be thrown into the sea. The liquors that are dispensed there had better be poured into the gutters of the streets."

Cause for alarm! The St Louis Republican says "there is one saloon to every 300 people in Missouri, and reform of some kind with the power to stay the ravages of intemperance is a severe necessity.

A friend of temperance recently stole a march upon the people gathered at a wine banquet and made a temperance speech. The freeholders recently assembled in the extension of the county jail at Patterson, N. Y. to celebrate the expenditure of $30,000 for that purpose and to partake of a banquet provided by the officers of the board and the contractors. After drinking a number of toasts Judge Woodruff offered as a volunteer toast, "The Temperance Cause," and called upon H. H. Barterom to respond which he did by saying:

GENTLEMEN, I thank you for this invitation and I recognize its fitness. You have assembled to celebrate the enlargement of this jail, rendered necessary by the use of strong drink in which you are so freely indulging this day. Down stairs the cells and corridors are crowded with criminals who have but changed places. A few years ago they were respected citizens, some of them occupying prominent and responsible positions as those filled by yourselves, but they commenced as you have commenced and they continued as many of you are continuing, and to-day they are reaping the harvest in a career of crime, and paying the penalty with a period of punishment. At this moment another bottle was opened and Mr. Bartram said, I hear the popping of the cork. I listen to the merry voices and the praises you are singing to the infernal spirit of wine, but there comes to me a sad refrain from the prisoners cell who is shedding penitential tears over his folly, and accompanied by the still sadder wail of anguish uttered by the broken-hearted wife, worse than widowed through the traffic in strong drink, which as a judge in one of your courts said is the great promotive of crime, a traffic licensed by your votes and sustained by the patronage you are this day giving it. It is with inexpressable sadness that I discover that there can be found in Passaic county so many men with hearts so hardened, feelings so calloused, sensibilities so blunted, that in a place like this, under circumstances like these they dare raise to their lips that which depraves the citizen and endangers the State.

Rev. C. S. Woodruff says of the liquor dealer: "You try to make us believe your business is honorable. If it is honorable why do you seek to cover it up and screen it from the public gaze? Why those screens upon the windows and extra doors in front of your place of business? Why not leave your place of business open as the butcher and the baker and druggist. When my baker makes fine loaves of bread he puts it into the window in the most conspicuous place. When my butcher get a piece of beef that excites an appetite to look at it; he exposes it to public view. The grocer and the dry goods dealer have their stores open and their goods exposed. Why does not the liquor dealer do the same if his business is honorable. When you make a successful work why not expose it. When you have a man fixed up as only your business can fix him, why not lay him out where he can be seen. Why not put a pile of beer kegs on the sidewalk and lay the man on it and say I have been all day fixing him, for it takes all day in this lager beer business.

Just look at the bloat. To-morrow morning he may have a tremendous headache. Then put up another man and say, I fixed him up with brandy. It is more expensive at first, but the work is done more quickly. Then here is another: This poor fellow had not much money, so I gave him Jersey lightening and I have to turn him over every fifteen minutes for if I left him longer in one position the liquor would burn through and escape. Why not put their men out and say, there are the results of my business. Will you answer now? Will you answer in the public papers?

Dim indeed in mental vision must be the man who cannot see in every instance thus far related the awful truth that strong drink is degrading and ruinous in its tendency and results. But these instances cited are of a general or national character. Let us gather a few excerpts from various speakers and writers of a more personal character.

Mr. Gough says: "Call me what you will, I hate alcohol, and I pray God to give me an everlastingly increasing capacity to hate with burning hatred any agency under heaven that can enslave, imbrute and take away the best part of a man's life, and give him nothing but an awful black and fearful recollection to pay for it."

Mr. Talmage, in his sermon on "The Night Scenes in New York City," says: "Tell me a young man drinks, and I know all the rest. Let him become captive of the wine cup, and he is the captive of all other vices. No man ever run drunkenness alone. That is one of the carrion crows that goes with a flock. If that beak is ahead you may know that the other beaks follow. In other words, strong drink unbalances and dethrones and makes him the prey of all the appetites that choose to light upon his soul. There is not a piece of sin upon this continent but finds its chief abettor in the places of inebriety."

"There is a drinking place before it behind it, or a bar over it or under it. The officer said to me that night, 'You see how they escape legal penalty; they are licensed to sell liquor.' Then I thought to myself, the court that licenses the sale of intoxicating liquors licenses gaming-houses, licenses libertinism, licenses diseases, licenses death, licenses all crimes, all suffering, all disaster, all woes. It is the Legislatures and the courts that swing wide open this grinding, roaring, stupendous gate of the lost.

A gentleman in Waukesha, Wis., says: "I heard a leading citizen of Waukesha say last night, in the presence of a multitude, that "the city had received $1,000 this year for whisky or saloon license.

"As one of the results, I have held four inquests on the bodies of four men, who were all citizens of this place, and all died from the effects of liquor bought on the authority of these licenses! Two committed suicide, and two, father and son, lay down on the railroad track and were crushed by the incoming train. Four men, soul and body, for $1,000!" When will our people awake to the enormity of the sin they are committing in licensing people to sell rum?—*Lever*.

Rev. John Pierpont speaks with emphasis about license. He says to the saloon keeper: "Yes, you have a license, and that is your plea; I adjure you to keep it; lock it among your choicest jewels; guard it as the apple of your eye; and when you die and are laid out in your coffin, be sure that the precious document is placed between your clammy fingers, so that when you are called upon to confront your victims before God, you may be ready to file your plea of justification, and to boldly lay down your license on the bar of the Judge. Yes, my friend, keep it; you will then want your license signed by the county commissioners and indorsed by the selectmen."

The Lever publishes an article upon legal inconsistancy. It says: "How long will people not only tolerate but actually legalize these dens of bestiality in their very midst, to ruin their sons and fathers, and demoralize and degrade humanity? How long will they license the cause, then shudder and groan and weep over the sad and deplorable result? License schools of vice, pauperism, madness and crime, and then build pauper-houses, mad-houses, prison-houses, and scaffolds for their motley graduates? Pay the taxes imposed in consequence, and then again and again license the same accursed traffic which renders these expensive poor-houses, mad-houses, asylums and prisons necessary? Legalize the manufacture of rowdies, tramps, mendicants, marauders and murderers, then arrest, try, convict, imprison, or hang the wretched victim? Fire the magazine, restrain, and punish the explosion. Beautiful consistency, profound statesmanship this."

Dr. Guthrie, of Scotland, now dead, was a strong temperance man. On one occasion he expressed his opinion of whisky in these words: "Whisky is good in its place. There is nothing like whisky in this world for preserving a man when he is dead; but it is one of the worst things in this world for preserving a man when he is living. If you want to keep a dead man, put him in whisky; if you want to kill a living man, put whisky into him."

There is a deep tinge of sarcasm about these remarks; but sad, oh, sad it is, they are literally true.

The Chicago Inter-Ocean, a well known secular paper says : "If all drinking should cease, jails could be rented for warerooms and poor-houses would have to advertise for boarders. It is true that the saloonist and sample-room keepers would have a hard time, but it would be over balanced by the good time that would come to millions of homes, where would be heard loving voices instead of curses and blows and sobs of wives and children."

WHAT ALCOHOL WILL DO.—The Sanitarian tells "What Alcohol will do." Thus: "It may seem strange, but is nevertheless true, that alcohol, regularly applied to a thrifty farmers stomach, will remove the boards from the fence, let the cattle into his crops, kill his fruit trees, mortgage his farm, and sow his fields with wild oats and thistles. It will take the paint off his building, break the glass out of the windows and fill them with rags, take the gloss off his clothes and polish from his manners, subdue his reason, arouse his passions, bring sorrow and disgrace upon his family, and topple him into a drunkard's grave. It will do this to the artisan and capitalist, the matron and the maiden."

What will whisky do for the health? is a question asked. Hall's Journal of Health, one of the most reliable authorities in this country, relates this instance: "A gentleman was arguing that a glass of brandy wouldn't hurt anybody. 'Why,' says he, 'I know a person—yonder he is now—a specimen of manly beauty, a portly six-footer. He has the bearing of a prince, for he is one of our merchant princes. His face wears the hue of health, and now at the age of fifty odd he has the quick, elastic step of a young man of twenty-five, and none are more full of mirth and wit than he, and I know he never dines without brandy and water, and never goes to bed without a terrafene or oyster supper, with plenty of champagne, and more than that, he was never known to be drunk.' "

Lo, here is a living example and disproof of the temperance twaddle about the dangerous nature of an occasional glass, and the destructive effects of a moderate use of liquors.

The Hall's Journal of Health makes this reply: "It so happened that this specimen of safe brandy drinking was a relative of ours. He died a year or two after that of chronic dysentary, common end of those who are never drunk nor ever out of liquor, He left his six children; he had ships at every sea, and credit at every counter, which he never had occasion to use.

"Four months before he died—he was a year in dying—he could eat or drink nothing without distress, and at death the whole alimentary canal was a mass of disease. In the midst of his millions he died of inanition. But this is not half. He had been a steady drinker, a daily drinker, for thirty-eight years. He left a legacy to his children which he did not mention in his will. Scrofula had been eating up one daughter for fifteen years ; another daughter is in the mad-house; the third and fourth of unearthly beauty —there was a kind of grandeur in that beauty—and they blighted and failed and faded in their teens; another is tottering on the verge of the grave, and only one is left with all the senses, and each of them is as weak as water."

A drunkard bemoans his fate. He says: "What a fool I am. Will these limbs that now tremble like an aspen ever again be steady? Will this burning fever be quenched? The ample fortune my father gave me is gone with my health and happiness, where demons in human shape deal out destruction in the wine cup. Is there no revenge? No, no, no; I am my own destroyer, and they—the wretches who have swept away my all—have protection of law, covered by a license granted by my own native State, but no protection for me and my starving wife and children."

But this ruinous rum traffic has its pathetic side. Incidents so unutterably pathetic as to make the angels weep could be multiplied by the thousands.

The widow of a Baptist deacon, who died four years ago, said to the editor of a Richmond paper a few days since: "The great mistake of my husband's life was leaving $200,000 to his children. My eldest son had not been in possession of his portion six months before he had acquired intemperate habits, and to-day, wrecked in health, and morals, he hasn't a dollar left of the thousands his father gave him. My daughter married an immoral man, who has spent her portion, and now her life is sad and dreary. It would have been a thousand times better had my husband left his means more largely to education and Christianity..

Prof. Goodrich says: "I had a widow's son in my care. He was heir to a great estate. He went through the different degrees of college, and finally left with a good moral character and bright prospects."

But during the course of his education he had heard the sentiment advanced which he supposed was correct that the use of wines was not only admissable but a real auxiliary to the temperance cause. After he had left college for a few years he continued respectful to me. At length he became reserved. One night he rushed unceremoniously into my room and his appearance told the dreadful secret. He said he came to talk with me. He had been told during his senior years that it was safe to drink wine, and by that idea he had been ruined.

"I asked him if his mother knew this; he said no; he had carefully concealed it from her. I asked him if he was such a slave that he could not abandon the habit? "Talk not to me about slavery," he said, "I am ruined, and before I go to bed I shall quarrel with the bar keeper of the Tontine saloon for brandy and gin to quench my burning thirst." In one month this young man was in his grave. It went to my heart. Wine is the cause of ruin to a great proportion of the young men of our country."

A drunkard made a will. Upon his dying couch he said: "I die a wretched sinner, and I leave to the world a worthless reputation, a wicked example and a memory that is only fit to perish. I leave to my parents sorrow and bitterness of soul all the days of their lives. I leave to my brothers and sisters shame and grief and the reproach of their acquaintances. I leave my wife widowed and heart broken and a life of lonely struggling with want and suffering. I leave to my children a tainted name and a ruined position, a pitiful ignorance and the mortifying recollection of a father who by his life disgraced humanity, and at his premature death joined the great army of those who never enter the Kingdom of God."

And there is womankind. Think what women have to suffer and silently endure because of this terrible curse of rum. In a most interesting address by the Rev. Cannon Wilberforce, recently, at Frome, Eng., he said: "Not long ago there was in my own parish one of the bravest, purest and brightest of the wives of workingmen I have ever seen. All through her married life she had been praying for bearing with and forgiving the man whom at the altar had sworn to love and cherish her.

"A short time ago he set his seal upon years of cruelty by raising his foot and kicking her savagely, and three hours afterwards she had gone 'where the wicked cease from troubling and the weary are at rest.' The last words she spoke were whispered in my own ear—'Don't be hard upon him when I am gone; he is so kind when he doesn't drink.' They laid the little form of her premature-born infant by her side, and four other little ones followed to the grave one more victim of the arch-fiend rum."

The Anvil, in speaking of "Drunkard's Wives," says: "If there be a lonely woman amid the multitude of lone and sorrowful women more to be pitied than another, I think it is a wife looking upon the one she has promised to honor lying upon the bed or floor with his hat and boots on; her comforter who swore at her as long as he could speak at all; her protector utterly unable to brush a fly from his face; her companion lying in the stupor of death, with none of its solemn dignity.

"As he lies there entirely unconscious, I wonder if she never employs the slowly passing moments in taking down her old idol, her idol from its place in her memory, and comparing it with the broken and defaced image before her. Of all broken idols scattered into fragments for the divine patience of womanhood to gather together and cement with tears, such a ruin as this seems the most impossible to mold anew into any form of comeliness. And if there is a commandment seemingly impossible to obey it is for a woman to love a man of whom she is in deadly fear, obey a man who can't speak his commands intelligently."

The theory of recognizing ones friends in a future world is a beautiful one and worthy of much thought, but I think it is commendable to try to keep them in a condition to recognize us in this world, try to keep a man while he is alive so he will know his wife and children, and not, as often occurs, turn them out into the storm on a winter midnight, or murder them in his frenzy.

One more brief citation and I am done. What does the rum traffic cost us besides blood and tears and sorrow, waste of time broken hearts and blasted lives? Besides all these what does this traffic cost us in hard cash.

About two billions a year in one way and another. Some paper in speaking of the reign of rum, say, "If the people of this country had to pay two billions of money every year to sustain a king over them, who squandered their property, corrupted their young men, debauched their daughters and destroyed nearly one hundred thousand of their lives annually in ruinous woes, they would rebel. The people of this country do pay that amount every year to sustain a despot who does all this; and instead of rebelling against his authority, they vote—a large majority of them—to put his servants and satraps over them.

I have quoted briefly from various Authors upon this solemn and awful theme of intemperance. I have added no comments to the incidents cited and the views expressed, and I ask, Do they need comment? Are they not complete and powerful arguments as they stand? And I can say of this lecture, as I could not have said had I expressed my own thoughts and views only, it is a great lecture, great in power and scope. There is not a man or woman who has listened to it to whose heart and intellect has not been carried with irresistible force the convictions of the awful truth that strong drink is degrading and ruinous in its tendency and results.

If that is true, you say, how long, if perchance forever, are we to endure this blighting evil that prevails throughout the land? But I answer that is a subject for another lecture, yea, it is a question to be settled in the ages to come. I close with a few words upon this subject from Rev. Henry Ward Beecher. He says: "The time will come when the temperance men will have it all their own way, but that time is far distant. The growth of temperance must be identical with the growth of the moral integrity of a country, and that is necessarily very slow. We have to eliminate those brutal characteristics which descend to us from a quadraneous ancestry that is not yet sufficiently remote. When we have put it a few centuries further back, men and women shall be evolved, who shall be but little lower than the angels. Not until then, not until the human race shall have risen above the plane of animalism, not until we shall have learned more of the divine life and the hidden life with Christ Jesus the Redeemer of the world, will the evil of intemperance disappear from among the Nations of the earth.

"Whose Shall the Triumph Be?"

HIS brief sentence perhaps more than any other, suggests or propounds a question which in its application to the temperance problem of to-day affords a theme for discussion of peculiarly impressive interest. We are alike one and all interested in the solution of this mighty problem before the people, which bids fair to shake this continent and send vibrations throughout the world. We have a wish to peer into the future as far as our visions can penetrate, to see and to determine as near as possible, what are the prospects of accomplishing this great moral reform of prohibition upon which the people have their hearts set. To determine the prospects before the work is accomplished, in a measure nerves the soldier in the sacred cause for the conflict. The chivalry of the soldier must be maintained by the hope of victory. No army will ever wage a successful battle if its General is the leader of a forlorn or abandoned hope.

Then if we accomplish nothing else in an hour's study of this theme we may spend it interestingly and profitably marshalling what evidence we can find favoring the view that prohibition will soon be an accomplished fact. We observe first that "Eternal vigilance is the price of liberty." This is one of the sublimest sentences, as well perhaps the profoundest truths ever uttered. While my faith is strong in the belief and prospects of the moral and religious elements of society to effectually accomplish prohibition in the face of hostile opposition I recognize that when this great reform is effected, it will require eternal vigilance to guard and protect the priceless possession we have secured. The liquor traffic is an Enemy which, when defeated, driven out of our country and made an exile in some forsaken spot of earth, will need to be guarded by a standing army, that our shores may be protected from its subtle intrusion. But we have not conquered this enemy—strong drink—much less have we driven it out of our borders; and we need not talk at present about a standing army to guard our shores after it has been exiled.

But we will confine our thoughts at this time to the prospects of these great accomplishments. Thirty years ago the work of temperance reformation practically and actively began in this country. About that time in the history of America the better thinking element of our people began to vividly realize that it rested upon them as a moral obligation to attempt to stay the

tide and ravages of intemperance as it was then sweeping as a tidal wave over
the country. It was a new work and a new departure for the Christian people
of America. Up to that time the people had been accustomed to free rum.
Those whose hearts and principles led them into that channel for a livlihood
had full sway in the manufacture and sale of stong drink, and the ravages of
drink, though not comparable with what it is to-day, were not restrained or held
in check by any power or influence. Free from all restraint the vicious and
debasing character and tendency of the liquor trade quickly developed into
the giant monstrous curse which we recognize it to be to-day. The evils of intemperance had spread as a mighty consuming fire from the length to the
breadth of our Nation. The blighting and debauching tendency and effect of
drunkenness upon the lives and morals of men, had burned deep its traces
upon the Christian civilization of America. Those lurid dens of human misery, wretchedness and woe, which we call drinking saloons, were being established in every town and hamlet in our land. The liquor traffic had assumed
alarming proportions. The king of evils and terror had exalted to a throne
and had swayed his sceptre of ruin over the lives and homes of the people
throughout the domain of our fair land. So destructive and farreaching was
the result that intemperance became recognized as a dangerous foe, and a menace to Christian civilization. A Christian public sentiment sprang up to battle
with this malignant power that was corrupting society, blighting the morals of
men and destroying human life. From that day to this those forces have been
contending, fighing a fierce and tragic battle upon the broad plains and'expansive fields of this great continent, and while no signal victory has been won,
to-day more than in the past is there encouragement to wage this battle to a
cruel termination.

It is important in this connection to note one weighty fact. It is this:
The reign of rum and its evil influences had greatly the start of temperance
societies and organizations. It was, so to speak, a thousand leagues in the
lead, before a sentiment favoring the suppression of the rum traffic had started
on the race. The liquor traffic had developed, as did slavery, into a formidable evil and became deep-rooted in the soil of our Nation before a moral sentiment was aroused, and before it was thought necessary to oppose its progress by
a systematized organization. It is important to understand this fact, as it has
a relation to the progress made by temperance societies. For the growth and
progress of temperance societies in this country covers a lapse of three decades
only, while that of the liquor traffic covers the lapse of centuries. And I am
impressed with the belief that if there is an honest reason to be given why
temperance societies have not coped with and destroyed the blighting evil of
intemperance, it is found in the fact that temperance societies did not undertake to handle this infamous business until it had developed into giant proportions.

Let us concede then that thirty years ago the war upon intemperance began. Also that the leagues of the rum traffic with their marshalled hosts were
camped upon the fields or arrayed in line of battle, and that temperance societies and temperance workers had just begun enlisting in an army to confront and withstand this battling foe. If these facts are conceded as substanti-

ally true, then thirty years of fighting has been done, on the one hand to maintain and to perpetuate the rum traffic, and on the other hand to suppress the evils of drunkenness and inebriacy. Which side has won the conquest? The answer is neither, but the battle is not over. The victory is neither lost nor won. Then the question is asked with a fresh and signal meaning—Whose shall the triumph be? And we ask ourselves the question, what progress has been made within the last thirty years in the endeavor by moral influences and moral implements of warfare to crush and to destroy the means of intemperance and to reform and reclaim fallen men throughout the wide domain of our Christian land. We answer a myriad agencies are in operation. A thousand channels have been opened up through which the electric current of vital influences are centered upon one object, that object is the destruction of the liquor traffic, the enactment of a national law prohibiting the manufacture and sale of the accursed stuff. This object and purpose, prompted by humane impulses, has been mapped out and carefully planned, and its speedy accomplishment is the heartfelt intention and desire of every lover of humanity and of God.

Perhaps the most signal success thus far achieved has been the progressive development of a public opinion demanding prohibition in the stead of license law. This is work well done, and established upon an abiding foundation. So much so that the more the dashing waves of the rum and whisky ring opposition beats against it the more firmly and immovable it stands. The sentiment of the American people demanding prohibition is as firm and abiding as if anchored to the rock of eternal ages. If there is one thing in our bright, happy country abiding, immovable and eternal in its character, it is that sentiment springing from humane impulses in every true Christian heart, that strong drink shall be banished from within our borders, and that the distillery, the rum-shop and the saloon shall not longer blight and wither by their scorching shadow the lives of all who are unfortunate enough to pass within the radius of their deadly influence. This feeling nestling within the hearts of men is interwoven with the warf and woof of Christian civilization; and the powers of hell and Satan cannot vanquish it.

One thing remains to be done by the people of our country it is to make this feeling, this sentiment, this principle, irresistable and overwhelming as the mountain avalanche of snow, which rushes in resistless furry down from its heights carrying terror and destruction in its descent. The feeling and principle of your heart is—the purity of the ballot box, education, religion, humanity, the advance of civilization, the progress and prosperity of our people and Nation, the best interests of humanity throughout the world, demand that the manufacture, sale and use of strong drink shall be prohibited by law. Then will you not act upon those principles, and instill those principles in the mind and heart of your fellow man, and will you not do this with an earnestness and zeal that will electrify and thrill those with whom your influence is felt. Will you not make the guild of your temperance principles so strict that in whatever circle you move your influence as an advocate and champion of temperance principles will be felt and recognized. This is an obligation resting upon every man, deserving the name of a Christian and a friend of temperance.

This sentiment and feeling that has had its growth and is maturing in the minds of our people, received its nourishing and fostering care, if it did not find its germinating power in the current temperance literature which has been dissiminated with lavish hands throughout the land.   Almost every book and newspaper, secular or religious we read contains some damning evidences of the awful consequences of strong drink.   This is true of the literature of to-day not directly associated with the work of temperance reformation.   The temperance literature proper is overwhelming with evidence convicting and condemning the liquor traffic as criminal and vicious in its character tendency and results.   The facts shadowing this infamous enterprise gathered from a thousand sources have been carefully prepared, compiled and published for circulation, and through this means the old and young in every part of the coun-country have become familiar with the fateful ravages and criminal records of universally prevailing drunkenness.

The influence of this means in awakening men to the consciousness of what intemperance is doing for America, and in converting men to the ranks of temperance workers has not been merely conventional, but it has been aggressive and powerful.   Temperance literature—though often sentimental and gawkish—has not been a failure.   Without it practically no progress would have been made in the work of temperance reformation, and in shaping influence and organizing methods and means by which the vital reform of national prohibition is to be hastened and accomplished.   Another vital influence and agency, to be favorably contrasted or compared with temperance literature in this work of reform, has been the temperance societies, lodges and organizations.   Their influence and work has largely been that of the Monitor steaming about the ports shelling the enemy whenever within reach.   Their work has been far-reaching, encompassing the universal domain by their influence. Their work has been practical, vital and effectual, as a great army so great that it cannot be numbered of reclaimed drunkards both in Great Britain and America stand ready to testify.   Thus far the work of temperance societies, has been the most practical and effectual of any agency that has offered a resistence to the spread of intemperance and the ruin of drink.   Wherever their influence has been needed they have went boldly to the rescue.   Under the clarion sound of their bugle have the army of temperance workers enlisted, and to the martial strains of their stirring songs are the veteran soldiers in this campaign marching on to battle, to victory and to triumph abiding steadfast and eternal.

The temperance pledge has rescued its millions from the brink of a plunging cataract where there is ruin and death.   Temperance societies, though often abused and held up to derision, have wielded the only influence that has checked the tide of intemperance and awakened a sense of alarm among those men who would engulf America in the vortex of drunkenness.   Its influence has been great, though not powerful enough to cope with the hideous-visaged demon of intemperance.   No power but that of constitutional prohibitory law, sanctioned by the suffrage of the people, will ever prove capable of doing this. Temperance societies have often checked and turned the tide of this evil of drink, but they have proved powerless to resist the mighty maelstrom of drunkenness which has deluged our land as the high seas deluge the shores of a continent. Of the many barriers that have been raised up to resist the tide of intemperance the temperance societies have proven the most effectual, but the dashing waves of the rum influence here and there has broken this barrier down and swept through, carrying destruction in its wake; and we are ready to ask what breakwater can withstand the surging tide of the rum influence and rum power.

Temperance societies and their concomitants have been a tower of strength in the work of resisting the spread of drunkenness and in planning and effecting the destruction of this foe to human happiness and human life, and if it is generally known among intelligent people throughout America today that intemperance, resulting from the prevalent sale of strong drink, is a monstrous evil, and that this evil is carrying wreck, desolation and ruin to the hearts and homes of our people; that knowledge, that familiarity with this state of affairs is largely, if not well nigh altogether, attributable to the ever-increasing power, scope and influence of temperance societies. If within the last thirty years any marked progress has been made indicating or pointing to the subsequent downfall and demolition of this king of evil and reign of destruction in our land, that progress is altogether attributable to the industry and activity of temperance societies. If to-day there is a force and latent power in public opinion that will yet rise up in its strength and grapple this demon of drink by the throat and destroy its life, that force and latent power has been generated by the salutary influence of temperance societies upon the minds, the hearts and the consciences of well-meaning people.

Next we consider briefly the power and influence upon the masses of public speeches or temperance lecturers; and consider it in relation to the progress of the temperance cause. And this agency is so intimately associated with the general work of temperance societies that it might properly have been considered under the same heads. The lecture bureau has been the artillery of the temperance societies. It has been a chosen implement of warfare with which they have fought their enemy and won their most signal victories upon ten thousand battle fields. It has been the thrilling, soul stirring speeches and lectures in the temperance halls, churches and at the forum that has formed public opinion, and has made it to glow with the brightness and splendor of a mighty consuming fire. The temperance speaker has invaded every realm in search of thought of logic of facts and of information, bearing upon this theme of momentuous interest, and has gathered together the results of his research, and used them as the General uses his mighty Battallion in the seige of battle to slay to destroy the defeat. It has been the influence of public temperance speeches, lectures and sermons that has agitated and swayed public opinion as the tempest moves the billows of the sea; and they will yet disturb the mighty depths of public sentiment until their influence shall shake the foundation of society and overturn human government, that it may be rebuilt and re-established upon safer and better principles. The evils of intemperance and reign of rum cannot always resist and withstand the power and influence of a public sentiment aroused by the damning record of dark crimes and treacherous villainies—springing from the source of intemperance—and which are constantly being brought to light and held up for the world to view. This is eminently a talking age, and a great army of men and women throughout America have set to work to talk down intemperance, and it is pretty certain that they will succeed. One thing is certain—their voice will not be hushed in silence while the wail of sorrow, of suffering and of distress arises from the homes of half a million drunkards in America. The people from the lecture platform shall know the truth and the whole truth about the wreck and ruin wrought by this pestilential curse of drink, and then when the time comes they can and will act as their hearts and consciences dictate about the suppression of this towering evil.

Let us now ask the question and answer it by clear, logical thought and candid reason. What are the prospects of suppressing the liquor traffic by the moral power and influence of the ballot, and winning the triumph in this moral conflict over these men who are striving to perpetuate in free America this ruinous traffic of drink? In discussing this great problem we observe first, that the men who discuss this problem and the men who lend an ear to its discussion are men who love and fear God, and have an abiding faith in the religion of Divine Revelation and the force, the power and triumph of the eternal principles of truth and justice; and in discussing the problem of the liquor traffic, which is all darkness in and of itself, we will gladly turn our eyes from the dense mist and darkness enveloping such an enterprise, and look toward the gleaming light which Christian civilization sheds upon the world, and with which our pathway through life is made resplendent; and how precious the thought that we have this blessed beaming light of Christianity to lighten our darkened pathway. We constantly blunder, stumble and fall when walking in its light, and how poorly would we journey along without its divine rays, and how faint would be the hope of ever accomplishing the reform of any abuse by which humanity is suffering to-day.

To my mind the prospects of accomplishing prohibition throughout our union of States is not a dim or vague conception of a remote possibility. Viewed in the light that Christian civilization will yet establish and maintain the universal supremacy of power and influence over the affairs of mankind and of earth, that it will master opposing influence and dissipate or bring under subjection every power of evil that tends to minish aught of its lustrious glory viewed in such a light it is not a subtlety or uncertainty that the blighting evils of intemperance shall disappear as mist in the sunlight of this burning consuming power. Men generally will not believe this, but to my mind this truth is as clear as a crystal. It is a plain simple problem as to whether temperance or intemperance shall win. It is easy to solve as a problem in division. It simply resolves itself into this, is the Christian civilization of the nineteenth and the near approaching twentieth century going 'to triumph over opposing obstacles, and win the conflict it is now waging with the powers of darkness and shed its sacred light over all the world, or is it going to fail and sink down in everlasting gloom. It is not understood and believed that Christianity has the power to eliminate the evil and vicious from society and destroy it, and that that power is augmented each day that comes and passes; and that in the sweep of ages that power will enevitable effect great moral reforms. You meet a man who drinks, and he will tell you that the liquor traffic will never be suppressed, but if you question that man closely you will find that his idea is that civilization will always remain what it is to-day. That the Christian and progressive civilization of this age is incapable of further conquests, that it has reached the zenith of its power. You will find that that man has no faith in the triumph of moral principles, and no faith in Christianity to elevate, purify and ennoble men and to lift mankind above the plane of vice, crime, degradation and drunkenness.

Men struggle hard against the admission of that which stigmatizes their principles and their lives as infamous, and which brands their business as degrading, demoralizing and ruinous. Men fight against accepting as true that which blasts their reputation and incriminates their business enterprise and occupation. And by way of recrimination and with the object of shielding themselves, they turn upon their accusers with the avowel that they are hypocrits, charge that the principles they advocate are false, unworthy of credence, and rend their characters by unwarranted declarations and innuendoes. This is characteristic of men. The fact stands well attested. Men living criminal lives will shield their reputation at the expense of truth. Men engaged in an occupation or business at variance with honor and principle and debasing to mankind, will protect their interests and defend the course and conduct of their lives by branding as false deceptive and tyrannous every thing that opposes and hinders the free and untrammelled exercises of their liberty and rights. In the whole range of criminal life and conduct there is not one piece of crime so dark and lurid but finds its justification by the man who committed it. Men can stand the accusations of their conscience, but they cannot stand the accusation of the world, and the stern rebuke of justice. And to ward off these piercing shafts, they hold up counter accusations as a shield and protection. In the depravity of their heart they declare Christianity a failure. 'The man whose face is seamed and ridged with the fruits of vice says virtue is a failure. The bloated, besotted inebriate says temperance is a failure. The highwayman and the murderer says the law is a failure. The reckless violators of the laws of health says the science of medicine is a failure. Pope Pius the IXth said the civilization of the nineteenth century is a failure.'

Men willfully or through ignorance deliberately place themselves upon the wrong side upon these great questions that involve the most vital principles of human government, and then looking at them from their false standpoint declare that these great questions of social and political economy are a failure. Men who make such declarations are looking in the line or direction of their own interests and sympathies, and their declarations do not pass current for truth, and will not stand the test of ages. The declaration that civilization is a failure, or the belief that Christian civilization is incapable of evolving a loftier and purer social and political government for the race, is both false and absurd in the light of reason. Such views and opinions can emanate only from the minds and hearts of those who find gratification in the anticipated failure or defeat of these principles that are of such vital interest to humanity. In the broadest sense the wish is the father of the thought, and how often is that the case in the affairs of life. Pope Pius IX. would never have found it in his heart to have said that the civilization of the nineteenth century is a failure had he not in looking forward seen that the advance of civilization would prove the downfall and ruin of the Romish Hierarchy.

The interest of the Romish church required that the world should remain in ignorance and darkness rather than advance toward the radiant sunlight of Christian civilization. Therefore he desired to make it appear that the civilization of this century was a failure. Liquor dealers, distillers and saloon keepers desire to perpetuate their business of manufacturing and selling strong drink; their livelihood comes out of this business; their financial interest is wrapped up in it. For this reason they say that temperance and temperance laws are a failure, and that all efforts to suppress their business will prove a failure; and looking at this great agitating question of the liquor traffic from the view and standpoint of their interests and sympathies it is very natural for them to say that men have not the moral right to suppress it, and the moral right to suppress this great traffic and to turn a million of men out of employment by one mighty stroke of national legislation is a problem for serious consideration; but this great end is to be accompliseed by moral means, and the people of this country feel that they have a right to accomplish whatever they have the moral strength to accomplish. It is proposed to accomplish prohibition by the majesty of suffrage. According to the spirit and to the letter of our institutions of free government in times of peace all national questions and issues are to be decided at the ballot-box. The ballot-box is the soverign arbiter of a free people and a free government. It is there we test the moral strength of opposing parties and factions upon issues of national interest and import. Legal prohibition will never be accomplished while the liquor traffic element has the moral strength to resist the measure at the ballot box. If the time comes in the near future or in the distant future when they cannot do this, then it will be fairly and honorably right and just that a prohibitionary law shall be enacted to take the place of the license law and the liquor traffic shall be suppressed. Again I repeat that the people of this country feel and claim that they have the right to do that which they have the moral strength to accomplish at the ballot box. This is a great moral contest, and if the friends of strong drink and of intemperance want to act fairly, honorably and manly let them marshal their men in full strength at the polls and by honest battle defeat the prohibition measure and not whimper about that the measure is morally and constitutionally unjust and unfair.

It is a matter of no very great weight or concern whether the champions of strong drink and of the beastly liquor traffic in general, credit or discredit the moral right and the ability of the temperance people to declare prohibition by legislation. The result will not be affected or influenced by their belief. Its accomplishment is an inevitable result. I admit it is a question yet to be settled in the future, but I claim that temperance principles and temperance measures are destined to triumph, because they are just and right and humane. This is the principle for which we are contending. This is the rock upon which we have set our feet. If anything succeeds in this world it is because it is just, and in exposition of this truth I love to quote the words of Carlyle. He says a man is safe in this universe, and invincible just when he joins himself to the bottom law of the universe. Which law he might have said is "justice." "Success," he says, "is not the criterion, but rather if the thing is unjust thou hast not succeeded. I tell you again there is nothing else but justice." In Past and Present the author says, "In this, God's world, with its wild whirling eddies and mad foam oceans, where men and nations perish as if without law and judgment for an unjust thing is sternly delayed, dost thou think that there is therefore no justice? It is what the fool has said in his heart. It is what the wise, in all times, were wise because they denied, and knew forever not to be. I tell thee again there is nothing else but justice. One strong thing I find here below, the just thing, the true thing;" and again he reiterates, "if the thing is unjust thou hast not succeeded." In speaking to Mr. Smalley, of our civil war, Mr. Carlyle said, "you were the stronger at last, you conquered, and you know people will have it I said, 'might makes right.' Suppose I did say it, I knew what I meant by it, not what you think I meant. There is a real true meaning in it. A man is an Atheist who believes that in the long-run what God allows to triumph is not the right." Again he says, "The wrong may succeed for a day, but let them be at it for years and justice will triumph." How firmly he stood for the defence of this great truth, greater than which there is none in the world. If we cannot depend upon the triumph of the right, then we have nothing to depend upon. I ask for no firmer rock upon which to stand. It is immutable as adamant, and this principle—the triumph of the right, the survival of the fittest—is the standard by which the cumbrous and blighting curse of intemperance, and the sale of strong drink is to be measured, tested and forever decided and settled. It is being, and is to be, made a political issue and decided by the dignified and tranquil means of suffrage. There is nothing wrong in is. If in time it fails, it will deserve to fail. If it succeeds, it will be because it is just and deserves to succeed ; and what is more, the interests of the temperance cause is going to be intimately and inseperably associated and linked with the destiny of Republicanism. The party of successes and of a thousand triumph is going to take this great issue upon its broad shoulders and bear it, and bear it on to success.

Commonly intelligent men have said, "Keep temperance out of politics," and they shrink with a devout horror from the thought that the Sunday law is going to be made a political issue, and that this mooted question is going to be settled at the polls and by the ballot in the hands of free voters; but not deprecation, however sincere, of these things will prevent their speedy accomplishment. This is the tendency and drift, and the organized influences of the whole universe cannot prevent it. It is but a question of another decade that will have an enforced Statute and Constitutional Law protecting the sanctity of our Sabbath, and shielding the sacredness of our Holy Religion. But men say that is not desirable. We have seen the evil consequences of a State Religion, and we dread the thought of such a thing ; but I answer, that is your mistake; it is because you do not understand it. A State Religion is not only admissible, but it is right, and will be an inevitable achievement of the near future. Mark my prediction. You cannot keep temperance, you cannot keep the Sunday question, you cannot keep religion out of politics. A State Religion will be the key-stone in the sublimely proportionate structure of the Christian civilization of this enlightened and independent republic. This is the tendency. A struggle will be made for this accomplishment. If it succeeds you will find in its success a warrant for its triumph, an evidence of its justice and a test of its orthodoxy. You say I revolt at the thought of such a thing as a State Religion, but you forget the rule and principle—if the thing is unjust it will not succeed. It is to be accomplished in the ages to come. If it is unjust it cannot be accomplished. This principle rules the world. It is the foundation law of the universe and the destiny of the race is safe in the hands of the race by reason of the perfect working of this law. It is safe to repose confidence and trust in this principle which rules and controlls the destiny of the race. While this principle is operative the world cannot go wrong. Its silent power and influence is felt in all the affairs of earth. Individuals, as well as Nations, can testify to this. Upon every hand we see the triumph of the right. Throughout the world this principle rules, silently yet irresistably. The right, the just, the true alone can succeed. Pretty soon you will discover that there is nothing but justice.

The Statesmen of the world are divided upon the question as to whether a Republican or Monarchical form of government is best. The ablest of them both in America and Europe claim that a Republic is the ideal Government, as it promotes intelligence, assures equal rights and guarantees civil and religious liberty to the individual. The Nations of Europe in the main do not believe this, and therefore do not adopt a Republican form of Government. But if in the lapse of ages the Monarchies and Kingdoms of Europe go down before the breath of these sublime and eternal principles of truth in National Government as the decayed trees of the forest go down before the breath of the tempest, the result will prove that Monarchical form of Government was wrong and that Republican form of Government was right, and from this decision, ruthless and intolerant thought it may seem there can be no appeal, and this principle is applicable in all the affairs of life whether individual or National in their character. I am a friend to political parties and religious sects that can win triumphs and conquer foes and establish the principles and truths they maintain upon a foundation that is abiding steadfast and eternal. I believe this can be done, and I believe that human justice is that unchangeable and unfailing foundation rock. If the foundation abide unshaken we find in that an evidence that justice was the corner-stone of the structure. There is a providence in this. There is a divinity that controlls the destinies of religious sects and political parties and rules in all the affairs of men, of Governments and of Nations. But even that divinity which controlls the destinies of men of parties and of Nations, is subject and tributary to this immutable law of the universe, "justice alone can succeed."

I believe that if a political party in our enlightened country and in this advanced age comes into power and maintains the unkroken supremacy of power for a given period of time, that its success will demonstrate the fact that it is right. Right in righteous principles, motives and character. A great many men are clamoring for the defeat of the Republican party; the party of success, the party that has done more to solve the problem of free government than any political organization that ever existed. They say it is corrupt, that its policy is wrong, that it mismanages the affairs of the Nation, and that the interest, safety and perpetuity of our national free government demands its defeat and overthrow. Personally I would say to these men: "Try your strength." If you are able by fair means to overthrow the Republican party upon the charges that it is corrupt and incapable, do it by all means. And your success will demonstrate the truthfulness of those charges. And the defeat of the Republican party will prove that it is wrong, and has been wrong in the past. But if after years of fruitless endeavor and effort those men disheartened and discouraged, abandon the undertaking and all hope of accomplishing this result, they will certainly admit that they made a slight mistake in their estimate and opinion of the party of success.

I know not why a political party founded upon the abiding principles of justice, of equal rights, of civil liberty, should not be as enduring as the world itself. I have this faith in Republicanism. I make this statement not so much to speak a good word for the political party which by its deeds of chivalry and loyalty has won my sympathy and admiration, as I do for the purpose of illustrating and elaborating this sublime principle which I have feebly maintained —the triumph of righteousness and justice. My closing thought is, we may confidently expect the triumph of the right, the just, the true. If we fail in our expectation we can take it for granted that the thing we considered right was wrong, and the thing we considered true was false. Carlyle, one of the master minds of the nineteenth century, reposed faith and trust in this principle. Then, cannot the friends of temperance anchor to that rock which the legions of Hell cannot shake or shatter, namely, "the eternal triumph of the right, the true, the just thing," and find in this principle an exhaustive answer to the temperance problem, "Whose shall the triumph be?"

General Phases of the Temperance Question.

o drunkard shall inherit the Kingdom of Heaven.—1st Corinthians. 6th verse, 10th chapter.

I do not propose to sermonize upon this passage of scripture but to indulge in a general dissertation of views and ideas upon the temperance issues of to-day. The language of the above text is startling and sad enough to cause the heavens to bend in pity for the rescue of the drunkard. It probably touches the worst feature of the case, yet there are many practical and personal features of this theme that come nearer home and which it is important to consider. The temperance question furnishes a wide range for discussion and theory. It is a great, and we may say, boundless field of which every foot of the soil is tillable; but after we have made the vast round and have touched upon all the living and vital issues that unbidden spring up in this great work of temperance reform, we come back to the language of the text, "No drunkard shall inherit eternal life," and without controversy but with sad hearts pronounce this the most painfully serious and important issue of all. For what shall it profit a man if he should gain the whole world and loose his own soul, or what shall a man give in exchange for his soul. The Divine Master told his disciples in one of his addresses to them to fear not them which kill the body but are not able to kill the soul, but rather fear him which is able to destroy both soul and body in hell. Now it is this worst thing that the terrible liquor traffic is doing for men it is destroying both soul and body in hell. It makes a clean work of it. A man cannot for a weary lifetime saturate, soak and defile his poor body with rum and whisky, thereby destroying it, without also defileing his soul and destroying it, and it seems to me that after a man has soaked his body in rum for a lifetime and finally dies, that perdition is about the most comfortable place he could get into. Surely he could not want to leave this scene of action, and go to Heaven, and mingle with saints and angels there. Yet, however, that was a very characteristic reply of the "lager beer Dutchman," who, when asked by a Christian man if he expected to go to Heaven, answered, "Yes certainly bye and bye, v'y not." But I have sometimes thought that the poor drunkard by the time he is ready —though not prepared—to die, has well nigh quenched all the longings of the soul for immortality, and that he would be glad to consign both his soul and body to the silent grave, that his soul might forever perish, and that his body might be consumed by the worms of the dust, and that his bones might mingle with the clods of the valley. But even this is denied him, and with the premonition of hell in his mind and soul he dies, only to awake to the awful realization of the fact that he is to live forever in the dark region of pain and woe appointed of God for the "Devil and his angels." Some men are foolish enough to preach the literal death of the soul. But to my mind the annihilation of the soul is simply inconceivable. It does not seem to me that God Himself—omnipotent though He is—could destroy the soul of man. Immortality is the divine attribute of the soul. In this respect the soul is divine and like God. The soul is a divine spark cast off from God. He may relegate that spark of Divinity to a region of darkness and sorrow, which he has fairly warned the wicked He will do; but I question in the very nature of things if it is possible for God to quench or destroy that spark of Divine life—the immortal soul.

If strong drink only had the power to destroy the body and leave the soul unharmed, it would not be so bad, but it inevitably compasses the destruction of both. Seventy-five thousand drunkards die in this country annually. Eight hundred thousand of this class of men throughout the world die annually. It is not the worst feature that these men sink down in the grave forever from sight. No, it is not that. But the worst feature is that upon the wooden slab at the head of each of their graves, you have to inscribe that most inexpressably sad of all epitaphs "no drunkard shall inherit the Kingdom of Heaven." This is the saddest feature. The drunkard lives a shrouded life here on earth, and when he comes to die he makes his bed in hell. Let those then who are engaged in selling this fiery liquid of death, and let those who are trying to overcome and destroy this accursed traffic, keep in mind the solemnly suggestive truth, that it has power to destroy both the soul and body of man in hell. It has all the power Christ ascribed to Satan himself. Yea it is an instrument in the hands of Satan for the destruction of men, soul and body.

But we are living in a materialistic age, and have to deal with a materialistic and an intensly practical people, and it seems well nigh out of place, if not improper or inexpedient to present the temperance question in this higher or spiritual light. It seems like an idle occupation or a waste of words to tell saloon keepers and the whisky venders of every class of to-day that by their bestial traffic they are sending the souls of men down to hell, and for that reason they should refrain from the deadly work. You cannot go into the saloon and use this argument, unutterably pathetic and deeply penetrating though it may be, with any degree of success. You cannot go into the halls of the Legislature of your State and make a successful issue upon this argument, nor can you in the Congress of the Nation with any propriety or with any prospect of success present and insist upon this feature of the case. Such an argument would only excite derision under such circumstances and in such places; but you must confine yourself strictly to the figures and tangible facts in the case. You may rehearse the formal statistics or the dark category of crime, of murder and of death springing from this source; you may even go before the counsels of the Nation and venture to tell something of the suffering, the woe, the poverty, degradation and shame that is bred and fostered by this accursed business on this side of the dark ford of death; but you cannot in this materialistic age take the mantle of faith and place it upon the shoulders of men and with them cross the swolen stream of death in pursuit of the drunkards spirit and penetrate the land beyond until you come to the place of outer darkness where you shall hear the "wailing and gnashing of teeth." No, that, the most appalling and terrible evidence of the awful curse of liquor is practically denied us, and the friends of temperance in perpetuating their work must principally con fine themselves to a practical and tangible line or course of treatment of this question of such painful interest and solemn import.

We must not cease to weep and pray over this temperance work. And if God refuses to hear and answer our prayers, then we may at once write in emblazoned letters the word "Despair" overarching all our efforts and all the yearnings of our hearts. But prayers and tears alone will not suffice. They alone will not usher in that day of promise and victory for which we long. And here we are reminded of the minister's reply to the deacon, who was weeping over the deficiency in one of their church collections. "Never mind weeeping," said he; "this church is no water mill, that it can be run with tears." And this is equally true and applicable in the work of temperance reform. The temperance issue is an intensely practical issue, and demands practical treatment. And if the friends of temperance are ever to achieve victory—decisive and illustrious—they must bare their arms and go forth as valiant soldiers nerved for the conflict, and by their valor deserve victory. And yet I cannot understand why the practical rather than the sentimental or religious element should preponderate in this great work of temperance. I mean by this that I cannot altogether understand why we are to take up the practical side of this question and present it to the people and to the authorities of the Nation, and not venture or dare to present the religious side. And yet this is true, and is made necessary by the conventional spirit or ideas of men upon this question. And yet this is Christian America; and this is the shadowy eve of the nineteenth century; and over the western hills we are beginning to witness the first appearance of the delicate tints and hues, that are but a prelude to the golden sunset of this glowing century. And sad, but true it is that the people of this country, with all their religious culture, grasp at the material and physical, and show no predeliction for the religious and the spiritual. If an effort is to be made to rescue the drunkard from a premature death and grave, it is out of some practical or sensuous consideration, rather than from a religious consideration. If the drunkard is to be ruthlessly deprived of the vicious indulgence of strong drink, it is because that he has a body that is being consumed by the burning liquid fire which is being poured into him, rather than because he has an immortal soul that is to be consumed in the lake of unquenchable fire. Alas how sad it is—especially when we reflect upon the prevalency of drunkenness—that "no drunkard shall enter the Kingdom of Heaven."

And yet peculiarly strange it is, that in Christian America, in the discussion of the temperance question as a political issue, this most distressingly sad phase of the question cannot be touched upon with any degree of propriety.

To my mind this condition of things is a striking commentary upon the God-lessness and Christlessness of our Statesmen and of the constitution of our Government. In this country the Church and State are separated from each other by a distance of ten million leagues, and maudlin Statesmen are continually holding up their hands in holy horror and crying out to the people to beware of a union of Church and State, to beware of giving the constitution of our government a religious complexion, just as if anything so gentle, so refined, so sweet and holy as the christian religion, would mar the symmetry, beauty and grandeur of the constitution, or bring reproach or disaster upon our Nation. Of the Statesmen who oppose a recognition of the christian religion in a constitutional amendment, I have this to say; one of two things are true, they are infidels or else they are not intelligently conscious or aware of what they are opposing. They simply do not comprehend the situation. The Church proposes the subjugation of everything in the world, including the government of Nations to Christ, and yet the Statesmen of this enlightened country want to keep the Church in abeyance, and deny its right to assert its power and influence in the affairs of the Nation. To my mind those men had as well be engaged in keeping back the tide of the ocean with a broom. I challenge that the kingdom of Christ is the leaven of righteousness that is to leaven everything in this world, and it will in due time leaven the politics of our government.

But let us again revert—if but for a moment—to the fact, that the conventional proprieties, ideas, and standard of modern times, seem to forbid that the soul's eternal ruin of the drunkard—which is the most appalling and terrible consequences of the rum traffic—should be used as an argument in the great political controversy and contest over the temperance issue. And it seems to me that there must be a reformation or change of conduct and views in relation to this phase of the subject before we can fairly get at the work of temperance reformation. Looking at the consequences of strong drink from the standpoint that its use involves and jeopardises the soul's eternal interests of a man, is looking at it from the loftiest and noblest standpoint. But in this advanced age, the people are too intensely practical, materialistic and Atheistic to present or consider the consequences of intemperance in this light. The temper and spirit of the age is this: If it is discovered that strong drink inflames the baser passions of men, destroys life and property, breeds crime, disaster and pestilence, it is perhaps best, as a matter of policy or political economy, that we suppress it by legislation. But it is rarely said: Let us suppress the rum demon, because he destroys in a burning hell the soul of a drunkard. And in treating the temperance problem I cannot refrain from setting up the standard of Divine Revelation, and saying, that the soul of the drunkard is infinitely the greatest consideration involved in this struggle. It outweighs every other consideration. For if the drunkard's soul cannot be saved from perdition, it is scarcely worth while to reclaim him from a drunkard's grave. And when I meet with men engaged in the temperance work, who question this proposition, I am tempted to doubt either their sincerity or their intelligent conception of the sacred import of the work they have in hand. Or, to clothe the same thought in different language, the temperance issue belongs peculiarly to the Christian people of America, and springs from Christian impulses. Underneath and back of this widespread and far reaching temperance movement is the great heart of Christ, and the will and impulse of God. And if you will investigate this matter carefully, you will find that there are but few, if any, men and women actively engaged in this Divine work who are not standing upon pleading grounds and interceeding terms with God, trusting in their faith to call down His blessing upon their work rather than trusting in their own strength to perpetuate and complete the great undertaking of temperance reformation.

There are a limited few however engaged earnestly in temperance movements merely from humanitarian motives, with no higher purpose in view than to relieve humanity from the suffering and sorrow inflicted by the blighting curse of strong drink in this world, but who never look forward to the awful perdition of ungodly men and to the suffering of the wicked in the world beyond this. But the answer comes back to this challenge from them, we are not committed to the belief that God is so unmerciful as to punish the wicked in the other world in the way in which the Bible teaches. Well then the Bible is a misrepresentation and is false, and I ask them if they will allow me to take the Bible out of existence, to sweep it from off of the face of the earth, utterly destroying it? No, they reply, we cannot take the responsibility and risk of destroying the Bible, for without it we might not be able to maintain the lofty standard of enlightened civilization to which we have attained with it as our text book, and after all it may be the word of God, a Divine revelation to man, shedding the light of Heaven upon his pathway. The point which I wish to make is this, it seems like a paradox, it seems to my mind extravagantly inconsistent for men to work with might and main to rescue men from the suffering and blighting curse of intemperance in this life without ever giving a thought to the awful peril to which they are subjecting their precious immortal souls in the world beyond this, and all this too in the face of overwhelming evidence that there is a perdition awaiting ungodly men. If it is humane, if the principle involved in alleviating suffering, solacing sorrow and protecting men from drifting upon the shoals of destruction in this life is right and commendable then how much more commendable and how much loftier and truer the ideal to guide, to guard, to teach men wisdom, touching their conduct, principles and beliefs that may involve eternal consequences, suffering sorrow and an endless death in the world beyond, and the question comes up to be answered again, if a man after he is reclaimed from dounkenness is to go on down to perdition, was it worth while to stretch forth the hand to save him from a drunkard's life and fate here on earth.

But as it were to rest our eyes, we will turn from this dark picture with its wierd and solemn shadows to look upon pictures—it may be—less sombre and sad. Let us briefly consider some of the phases of the dirge-like theme of temperance—of a more immediate and personal interest. We may profitably consider first, subjects that may be classed under the head of popular fallacies. First and notably is that glaring delusion, that selling destructive and destroying alcoholic poisons is simply an exercise of "personal liberty," forgetful of the fact that it is the province of civil law to check, restrain and to control the exercise of personal liberty. Viewed from a standpoint of cold formal reason it is simply a delusive fancy to enter the plea of "personal liberty" and claim and maintain it, as a justification for selling a lurid flaming poison to a man which it is known will excite the passions of hate, murder and darkling crimes, and which will also destroy life; and yet a man who has his means invested in such a business, and is getting his livelihood from such a source, will advance such a claim with a marked degree of gusto and nonchalance. Saloon keepers find a justification of their business in the argument that they are simply exercising a sacred liberty and right in selling that which destroys both human happiness and human life. But the favorite retreat of the whisky seller when he is attacked about the inhumanity and general bad character of his business is to dodge behind his "license," which makes his business legal in the eyes of the law. In an emergency he quickly produces his license and holds it up as if it were an invulnerable shield through which the arrows of truth and human justice can not penetrate and pierce him to the heart. But in this argument there is however this virtue, it is consistent, for the law that licenses the saloon does—whether it wills it or not—justify the accursed traffic of strong drink.

License law however is preferable to free rum. And license law when interpreted by the more intelligent classes of people does not necessarily mean or imply a seal or sanction of approval of the traffic of "ardent spirits," but it should be regarded rather as a compromise measure—a law enacted in a case of emergency or severe necessity, a legal measure enacted to restrain and limit the sale of rum at a time and under circumstances when the people did not demand, require or solicit the utter prohibition and extinction of the traffic. License is a travesty of justice. It is inconsistent. It is however not unjust, it is simply partial justice. But the whisky dealers take a lower and less intelligent view of the license law, holding generally that by the enactment of such a law the government sanctioned or approved of the liquor traffic. But this is clearly a mistaken idea. The Government, i. e. the people, enacted the license law simply because they could do nothing better. It is a primitive idea of reform effected at a time when the people neither had the discretion nor moral strength to effect a sweeping radical reformation. A riper age in the history of civilization will demand its repeal and the enactment of a better law in its stead.

As has been said, the saloon keeper is consistent in taking refuge behind his license as a bulwark of defense when wronged and injured humanity hurls the shaft of rebuke and censure at his heart. It serves him a plausibly decent purpose here in this world, but it will prove a transparent and brittle shield for the pretection of his heart in the great day of assize. The dealer's license can be written on a small parchment. But it would take volumes as great as an Encyclopedia to record the deeds of infamy and crime that spring either directly or indirectly from his business. In the great eternal day we may see the parchment and the volumes laid side by side for comparison. License is the law's guarantee for protection; and the saloon keepers of America, with their license in their hands, are as strong, secure and defiant as an army behind barracks. But there is no license law on God's statute-book.

The law of Heaven does not license so inhuman, debasing and destructive a business as strong drink. Neither will the law of humanity and justice—when after the lapse of ages it is purified and perfected—license such a business. The pitying wail and prayer of millions of broken-hearted wives and children continually ascending the skies from the drunkards' homes, will yet be heard at Heaven's throne, and God will send relief and redemption, and then the tears of joy from the eyes of the disenthralled wives and children falling upon the pages as they read our statute books will obliterate every trace of the infamous license law which so long has been the shield of the drunkard-maker.

Another popular fallacy is this: "The Government derives a large revenue from the whisky trade and manufacture. Its revenue from this source in round numbers is seventy million dollars annually. And this, whisky dealers say, is a plea, or excuse, or justification for the perpetuation of the business. When such an argument is advanced, it is an evidence of one of two things. Either the person who makes such an argument is deceptive or he is ignorant. Follow such an idea or proposition out to its legitimate conclusion or consequence and you will not find that it contains a trace of reason, judgment, sense or justice. Men of the whisky fraternity are always harping upon this one string: "Our business largely supports and sustains the National Government," heedless and forgetful of the fact that its dire consequences deluges our people in untold and unnamable suffering and sorrow, and unmindful and unconscious of the fact that the loss of property and life by accident, the loss of property by theft, the cost of prosecuting criminals, maintaining prisons, alms-houses and asylums, all directly traceable to and made necessary by the liquor traffic, in the aggregate cost our people thirty times more money than the amount derived from internal revenue on whisky and tax for municipal license. Besides, it is beneath the dignity of our grand Government that it should be sustained by money derived from such a source. But it is not necessarily true that the money derived from such a source is applied in such a way. The income of the Government is one hundred and fifty millions annually more than is necessary. The cost of maintaining the Government in 1882 was two hundred and fifty-seven million dollars, while the money derived from customs alone was three hundred and twenty million—seventy-three million dollars more than necessary for the actual expenses of the Government. So it happens that the internal revenue project—which was a war measure—can be abolished altogether without to any extent distressing the Government financially.

But let us emphasize this one thought that the best and the only practical way of abolishing the internal revenue abomination is by the legal prohibition of the manufacture and sale of liquor. For it would be facing about and taking a step toward barbarism and toward chaos to lift the burden of Government tax from off of the manufacture of distilled liquor and thereby license its free distillation. There may be a measure of injustice in the internal revenue business. Grant it that there is, yet it is infinitely better to curb and restrain the accursed liquor business in this way, than it would be to sunder every restraint and suffer the country to be flooded with whisky by free distillation. The same is true of the municipal State or National license system.

Anything unner the starry canopy of the firmnament is better and more desirable than free rum. If we cannot by legitimate means abolish the accursed traffic, then give us every legal restraint and power that will tend to curb and limit its influence and dark rolling tide of ruin and desolation.   There is but one true solution to the liquor problem, and that solution is "legal prohibition." But society is not ready for this arbitrary political measure yet.   Well, give us the next best thing, heavy government tax and stringent municipal license law upon whisky and the saloon that they may serve as a breakwater to their work of destruction.

But as there is no danger of exhausting this subject of license we may pursue it further profitably. Let us hear what others say upon the subject. Some writer clearly defines his idea upon the subject thus:

LICENSE LAW A FAILURE.—To license saloons is to license murder.

"It has been estimated that in the United States alone 75,000 die prematurely from drink every year. When we license the manufacture and sale of these drinks, we authorize the premature death of 75,000 of our people annually and make the saloon-keepers our agents to accomplish the work.   But these men object to being called murderers. These men engage in the work with full knowledge of the aggregate results. At least, most of them do. Those who license them to do this work, also know the results. They wantonly do this for money, in "disregard" of the rights or safety of others.   Hence it is murder, neither more nor less. If this work only murdered or assasinated men physically, it might be borne with.   I know it is terrible to think that there is a foe in our land that is killing 1,155 of our people every week, and still worse, that such a foe is licensed and protected in this deliberate slaughter by our law-makers, but the worst of all is the murder of character, manhood and morals.   Every one, too, who gives any attention to this question, knows this.   And yet, in the face of this evil and the knowledge of it, men who claim to be philanthropists, nay, even Christians will sanction it with their votes and clothe it with the authority of law.

We do in this as we would not do in any other evil.

If a man should come to us who is skilled in the black art, and advertise that he is competent to dement all our young men, and upon trial he should actually for a small fee, destroy the minds of fifty of our young men, would we think of licensing him to prosecute his calling in our community? Such a thought would be preposterous! He would not have wasted their fortunes, nor destroyed their physical manhood or shortened their lives, to think and reason. His work is not nearly so bad as that which is being done by the saloons, and yet no one would think of licensing it.

We prohibit the smaller crimes, and license the greater.

The power that makes is greater than that which is made, Now when we note the causes of fraud, theft, rape, fighting, brawling, killing, etc., we find that about ninety per cent. is properly put to the account of the sale and use of the rum. We license one man to make another man drunk, and then fine the man for getting drunk! We license the saloon man to craze the brain of one of his customers who kills another man as the result, and then we hang the man who killed the other, while he who really did the deed, or did that which caused the deed to be done is petted as a gentleman of good moral character and standing! Why can we not learn to be consistent and license men to get drunk and then do the work of drunken men, or else stop the iniquitous business altogether. What can we expect but failure as long as we continue to act thus sinfully?

We licence both the use and the abuse of drinking.

It is common for men to try to shield themselves from the consequences of the liquor, traffic, by claiming that they have only authorized the use and are not responsible for the abuse of these liquors. This will not do. Any beverage use whatever, is an abuse of intoxicants. This has been determined upon by the highest medical authority both in Europe and America. Here all science is agreed. Hence, when they licensed the sale as a beverage, they have licensed the abuse. But we have no need of making fine points on this subject. The truth is, when we license a saloon we license that which is everywhere done under that name. We license them to do what we know they will do by virtue of the authority we give them. But suppose that those who get drunk were the only responsible persons in the matter, what then? We know that they get drunk on drink, and that they get that drink in the institutions which we have sanctioned. Such has ever been the case, and such will be the case as long as we continue the same regime."

The Rev. Mr. Talmage puts himself on record upon this subject in the following forcible language. In answer to the usual argument that the traffic brings to the United States Treasury millions of dollars in the way of tax, he says: "I tell you where the liquor traffic pays the United States Government one dollar it steals ten in the property destroyed, in the criminal trials that are necessary, in the poor-houses, the alms-houses, the penitentiaries that are required to take care of the victims. The United States Government makes as much out of the rum traffic as you would make as a merchant if you sold a man a knife for one dollar, and after he had paid you the one dollar for the knife he should thrust the blade through your son's heart—as much as if you sold a box of matches, and after the customer had paid you for the matches he opened the box, and with the first match struck set fire to your dwelling."

And here is what another man thinks about the license system: "Hon. Emory A. Storrs puts the wole question of liquor license in a nutshell in the following supposed interview between the whisky man and the city of Chicago. The former says: "Give me for one year the privilege of scattering ashes upon the hearth-stone; give me for one year the privilege of sending the outraged wife into the streets from a blackened and ruined home; give me the privilege for one year of sending the youths along the highways of debauchery and crime, and I will pay the city fifty dollars," and the noble city of Chicago says, "Done."

Another popular fallacy that is abroad and which should be answered is this: Men interested in the distilling business and rum traffic claim that this business is as honorable as any other business, and should be treated like every other business. If this statement is true, it is true only when viewed from the whisky sellers standpoint. Such an assertion is certainly not intended for universal acceptation and belief. The thought that the liquor business is as respectable and legitimate as any other business is circumscribed by a narrow boundery and eminated from a small mind. Without making any nice distinctions or pointing out any specifications, divisions or subdivisions, it is the proper thing to say that the general character of the liquor traffic is bad, pernicious and disgraceful. The rum haunt where the slobbering drunkard is turned out, idleness bred, brawls fostered, bloody murder and darkling crimes instigated, plotted and executed, is not more honorable or legitimate as a financial business enterprise than is the pest house, the pool houses, the gambling hell and the houses of ill-fame. Eternal shame and infamy rest upon the name of the city or Nation that fosters licenses or tolerates any one of the institutions in the whole dark category. The man who professionally sells ardent spirits for a livelihood believes but that his moral character and humane principles are on a par with those of men of other professions and avocations. This strange freak of insanity has an analogy and a parallel in other things and in other directions. For instance the gambler believes that all men are gamblers in principles or would gamble if they knew how and could win. The thief believes that all men would steal if they had an opportunity and necessity pressed them. The murder whose hands are crimson with the blood of a foe or betrayed friend believes that all men are murders under certain conditions and provocations.

Thus men and criminals in whatever plight they are found try to adjust society to their own condition and circumstances, and in their mad effort destroy and break down every ideal of virtue and honor, and declare that all men are bad and wicked alike. And thus liquor dealers try to prostitute and degrade to the low level of the infamous liquor traffic every honorable, respectable, and legitimate business of which our proud civilization boasts. But intelligent men cannot be hoodwinked in any such a way, and all such sophistry is doomed to fail in the accomplishments of its infamous designs.

In corroboration of what we have said, we append two brief excerpts.

'The National Distillers' Convention held in Cincinnati, resolved that the entire liquor business must be treated "just like every other business." No, gentlemen. That will never be in this county. The liquor traffic is not like every other business. It is not like any other business. There is no other business in all the traffic and commerce of the world the total outcome of which, here and everywhere, as is the case with this business, tends to waste moral pollution, crime, woe, and ruin. Take the four thousand liquor saloons in Chicago. What a daily record is theirs, of temptation and vice, of impoverishment and crime, of character ruined, of hopes gone out in the blackness of despair, of blighted homes, of social disorders, and a comprehensive curse that touches, in one way and another, almost every person in the city. No, gentlemen of the distillery and the grogshop, this thing can not go on always. Society has some rights which even you shall yet find yourselves bound to respect.'

"I sell liquor for a living. I must live." 'If a man must live like a shark, swallowing the substance of others, he must take the chances of a shark. It is a question whether or not there is absolute necessity for such a man to live. If he voluntarily starves to death because he is too lazy to do anything but sell rum, then let prohibition make a martyr of him. A counterfeiter must live, but his boarding-house will be the State Prison if he is detected and proved guilty of tampering with the currency of the country. Is it not a greater crime to make counterfeit men than it is to make counterfeit money? The traffic in rum dilutes the pure gold of manhood and stamps the victim with the spurious mint mark that resembles humanity, while in reality it cannot be trusted. There is honorable work for honest hands, and there is no valid excuse for selling what Robert Hall called "liquid fire and distilled damnation" for a living; and a license written on paper or parchment will be a poor attenuated shield to hold up on the grand day of assize to keep off the arrows of Almighty wrath.'

Still another popular fallacy, and one which is akin to the one we have briefly discussed, is the anomalous difference in degree of respect which society makes between the wholesale liquor dealer and the saloon keeper. Society rules that the former is respectable and that the latter is disrespectable. The distiller, the man who manufactures the accursed stuff; the wholesale dealer, the man who sells it by the barrel and sends it out in great quantities through every avenue of commerce, society takes by the hand and pets and caresses as a gentleman. But the man in the low groggery, who is well nigh, if not altogether destitute of refinement, the saloon keeper who stands behind the bar and "puts the cup of poison to his neighbor's lips," and at whom the Bible thunders an anathema, is frowned upon and spurned by society, and rejected at the door of the church. This is manifestly an unjust deal. Consistency, reason, analogy, nor justice does not sustain any such ruling. The question of priority, of respectability as between the wholesale and the retail dealer of liquor, has been settled, nominally, by society. But the degree of difference between the two is so nice a distinction that the temperance people in their blundering rudeness cannot appreciate it. It does not appear to the candid, intelligent reasoner why the man who wholesales the liquid fire that burns up the bodies and souls of men should be regarded as a more ornamental, useful, honorable and respectable member of society, than the man who keeps a bar and sells the fiery poison by the dram. And yet society makes and sustains this anomalous distinction. And if an investigation were instituted it would be found that there are but few metropolitan churches but that are guilty of warmly nestling within their fold wholesale liquor manufacturers, merchants, and dealers, while the bar-tender or saloon-keeper, if he should apply, would be politely and with tears of regret refused, and turned away. But society, however, and even the church, is a poor arbiter to which to appeal for the decision of such a question as this. But there is this redeeming feature and saving clause, the better element of society and better order of churches do not make, sustain or tolerate this manifestly unjust distinction.

The age is rife with such follies· America is a hot house in which society has grown up and matured, and after all it is nothing but a mushroom. It is the poorest and meanest thing that has sprung up and ripened in the rich loamy soil of the cultivated garden of our free country. Society is a mongrel amalgamation of the good, bad and indifferent, especially the latter two. It, with a haughty mien and nonchalence, asserts its importance, but it does not authoritatively settle or rule in questions of merit or importance and exerts but little influence where just discrimination is sought. May God who holds the the destiny of worlds in his hand protect this country from the rule and domination of a flatulent, vaunting empty society regime. There is one other ruling of society—and one only perhaps—parallel with the one we have briefly discussed. The liquor scourge and the "social evil" of America are twin relics. The former championing bestiality, the latter championing obscenity. The parallel to which we refer is the distinction society makes touching the social and moral standing of young men and young women who are abandoned to lives of shame. In all large cities throughout the country young men, with a generous exception, to an alarming extent support houses of ill-repute. In the aggregate they support an army of one million fallen women in America. Society feigns to know no distinction of moral character between the man who leads such a life and the one who does not. But the unjust ruling of society to which we refer is this: A young man may persistantly and continuously pursue a course of shame and infamy during the lapse of the best decade of his life, and after he has run the round of social dissipation and crime and has sucked all that is palatable out of a life of shame can turn from the association of harlots and turn his polluted feet from the criminal way he has been treading and without even a semblence of reform and without a blush of crimson shame upon his cheeks, seek out and marry wealth, beauty and innocense. And society flocks to the mock burlesque and sacriligious marital ceremony, and with dazzling pomp and peals of merriment pays its respect, homage and well-wishes to the strangely blended, defiled and innocent twain.

But shift the scene, reverse the actors in this dark drama. Let a young man of passable moral standing leave the beaten paths of respectability and go into the paths of shame and seek out and mary an inmate of those haunts of infamy and watch the result. Society would spurn him for such an unholy alliance, and turn with devout horror and loathing contempt from the very contemplation of such a breach of its rights; and that young man would go through life wearing upon his brow a deeper mark of disgrace than the one which distinguished the murderous Cain, until the day of his death. The act would drape his life and his memory in eternal infamy. Are these things not true? I appeal to the judgement of every intelligent observer of society for an impartial decision, if these two picture are not true to life? Is not the former scene enacted every day in our large cities? and is it not true that the giddy, dazzling and fashionable worldly society of to-day morally, is corrupt to the core, and at the core, and does not society foster, cherish and encourage this corrupt, vitiating and demoralizing state of affairs? Society pleads innocence and feigns ignorance as to the actual status of the moral character of the young men who sustain it. But every person of intelligence and discernment knows that these things are only blinds, and that society is fully aware that the one thousand houses of disrepute in every large city, are supported and sustained practically, if not wholly, by the young men of those cities, and society is also conscious that those very young men pass current in every social circle for men of respectability and good moral standing. But it is time to roll down the curtains upon the dark and damning scenes of this awful, deplorable human drama. For the review or contemplation of such scenes of moral polution and obloquy that actually transpire in human society in this the evening of this grand Christian century shocks and paralyzes the sensibilities of all who make any pretensions to respectability and morality, and vitiates and depraves the pure in mind and heart.

But to revert to the theme in hand for discussion, is it not true that the distinction society makes between the man who wholesales and the man who retails liquor are parallel and alike unjust with the distinction society makes between the fallen woman and the young man who treads with her the path of shame? It is indeed a strange commentary upon the Christian civilization of this country, that such corruption and moral pollution in society should exist, and that such manifestly unjust rulings of society should be tolerated or should be possible. But despite of what religion has done for the world, humanity has sunken very low into the mire of sin and moral degradation.

We are living in a startling age. We are living in an age when the carnival of vice and crime runs riot and rampant, when the mora. sensibilities of men are blunted by the prevalence and viciousness of sin, when the convictions of honor, justice, rectitude and propriety have been blurred and the conscience seared by familiarity and contact with every shade of sin and infamy. The partition wall that separates virtue from vice, that separates the exalted and refined from the vulgar and debased, has been broken down, and the good and bad flow together, and the honorable and dishonorable in society mingle, intermix and interlace without a thought of the propriety of distinction and appropriateness.

Still another fallacy is this: in communities and sections where temperance people are crowding the liquor sellers to the wall it is proposed to raise the price of license to five hundred dollars. This is of course a compromise measure. If the revolt of the temperance people against the awful scenes of crime perpetrated in the name of liquor becomes too strong and threatens defeat—the liquor dealers propose as a compromise measure to raise the price of license double and thereby reduce the number of saloons one-half. This at best is but a flimsy measure of relief.or reform. It may be adopted and may come into practical operation for awhile, and serve the purpose for which it is designed—that of delaying legal prohibition, but it is not a wise movement, and will serve no worthy or permanent purpose. It is not a measure that should elicit the support or co-operation of the friends of temperance. The temperance people are contending for a principle. And if they do their duty they will remain restless and discontented as long as one individual saloon infests the country. Reducing the number of saloons one-half in America is not necessarilly a temperance victory. The patronage of the poorer class of saloons and low groggeries that will necessarilly be weeded out by this new regime, will flow into those saloons, that are permitted to remain. And this increase of patronage will enable every dealer to make his saloon an alluring palace and a gilded Hell. And raising the price of the license double will only necessitate his doing a larger business to cover the increase of expense.

Even if the number of saloons should be reduced four-fifths from the number that now exists, it would not necessarilly affect the present enormous

daily consumption of liquor.   Men who have a thirst for liquor, will have it,
if the accursed poison is in sight, or is to be had by any effort or at any price.
Drive out the low groggeries by an increase of license, and the tendency will
be to make the saloon business more respectable by making such haunts of
infamy and lairs of ruin more attractive and gaudy.   By making every saloon
palatial in its appointments, embellished with everything that money will buy,
you pay a premium upon this infernal traffic that brutalizes men and degrades
society.

So far as the moral influence upon society is involved, the third class
saloon and groggery is not necessarilly more debasing than the gilded haunts
where the lurid liquid poison is dispensed.   And the man who is a temperance
man from principle is just as uncompromisingly opposed to its being sold at
one place as the other.   Besides, is it a fair, honorable and just deal to starve
out and drive to the wall the poor men who are struggling for an existence in
this nefarious business, by transfering their rights and privileges—the bloated,
besotted drunkards' patronage—to a more favored and fortunate class of whisky
sellers.   This compromise measure of increased license will not do.   It is an
unprincipled movement.   It is not honorable to compromise upon anything
that is wrong in principle, and rotten at the core.   There can be no choice
between two rotten apples.   The only right thing is to reject them both.
Whoever conscientiously believes, or whoever affects to believe, that raising
the price of license and diminishing the number of saloons will obviate the
the necessity of pushing legal prohibition to its legal consequences is pursuing
a weird and strange phantom.   You cannot adjust any evil to society.   You
cannot ameliorate or modify any positive moral evil so that it will not be
offensive to society, or so that it can be established on a permanent and
abiding basis.

The only true solution to the great temperance problem is prohibition.   If
civilization should evolve men as pure as angels, at one extreme it would be
all the more marred by drunkenness at the other extreme, even though the
drunkenness should be only occasional, and it will take many centuries for
evolution to produce a race of men so pure and elevated morally that none of
them will be subject to the temptation of drink when such temptation
are thrust before them in enticing and alluring forms.   And the purer the
order of Christian civilization the more sensative it will toward intemperance
even though it be modified and infrequent.

Here we naturally and almost unconsciously drift into the consideration
of another fallacy, closely related to the one we have been discussing.   It is
the phantasmal and delusive idea, that as civilization advances and improves
that the great whisky enterprises of the country will adjust itself, so that it will
not be necessary to control it by Legislation, or necessary to Legislate against
the wishes of the people touching the question of what they shall eat or drink.
That in some way or other, in a way not discernible, the worst and most
distressing features of rum drinking will yet gradually disappear, and the
temperance people become reconciled to its sale.   Or, that without the interference of Legislation, the sale of liquor will gradually decrease as the population of the country increases; or that after awhile whisky will not intoxicate

or addle men's brains; or that in the event of time men will not murder their fellow men when maddened by the inflaming power of drink. But not since the day of Esop's Fables, or the day of the appearance of the serpent in the Garden, has there been whispered into the ears of men such dulcet strains of delusion and deception. Such gauzy, transparent arguments as these are shields, held up to ward off the javelin thrusts of truth, hurled by the dauntless soldiers of the temperance legion. Human nature always has, and ever will remain the same. Intemperance, as far back as either sacred or profane history takes us, has always been distressing in its effects and results. And as far back as history reaches, men have always had a weakness for inflaming drink. And it is a wierd fantasy to suppose after the lapse of fifty or sixty centuries that the next generation of men will not take as naturally to inflaming drink, as the birds will to flying in the air, or the fish to swimming in the lakes and seas. . Most certainly the next generation of men, even to a greater extent than this generation, will be a race of drunkards, if it so happens that whisky shall remain a purchasable article. For the benefit of those whose feeble brains are infatuated with the idea that the awful scourge of whisky selling will adjust, or take care of itself, and that intemperance will by degrees diminish, and that its most offensive and harrowing features will gradually disappear, we quote some statistics.

First, we note that at the present time there are eighty million gallons of whisky in the warehouses in the United States, a gain of seventy-three millions in eleven years. Enough to confirm two million of drunkards, allowing forty gallons for that purpose to each individual man, and that is a generous allowance.

But for fear some ingenious whisky dealer should controvert or upset this argument we offer in corroberation of what we have said the following table of statistics:

"The report just issued from the National Bureau of Statistics shows a steady increase during the past five years in the consumption of liquors in this country. The consumption (not manufacture) of distilled spirits during the years 1878, 1879, 1880, 1881 and 1882, respectively, were 57,111,982, 54,278,-475, 63,526,694, 70,607,081, and 73,556,036 gallons. For the same year the consumption of wines, native and foreign, was 19,812,675, 24,532,015, 28,-484,428, 24,231,106, and 25,628,071 gallons. But the chief increase has been in malt liquors, which aggregated 310,653,253, 345,076,118, 414,771,690, 444,806,373 and 527,051,236 gallons."

And then there are those who hug the dulusion that light wines and lager beer will eventually take the place of the use of strong liquors. And that in that way intemperance and its horrible consequences will be diminished. This theory is deceptive and misleading in both its bearings. In the first place the foregoing table of statistics does not support the theory that the use of wine, beer and ale are tending to diminish the use of liquors, and in the second place the theory cannot be established, that the same destroying consquencees that spring from the use of liquors does not spring from the use of wine and beer. Either one will intoxicate, and the intoxication caused by the use of one is the same as that caused by the use of the other. And if we should investigate this matter carfully we would in all probability discover, that greater harm and injury arise from the use of wines and ales than arise from the use of liquor, for the tendency in the use of milder beverages is to go to excess, not fearing or apprehending the consequences until too late.   It is my conviction that the wine glasses and beer mugs are more alluring and fatal to young men and young women than are those dainty glasses in which the most ardent spirits are served.

Let those who question the intoxicating and deplorable effects of wines and beer read the following incident:

"WILL BEER INTOXICATE?—They say that beer does not intoxicate ; that it promotes health and happiness, and if its use should become general, would redeem society from much of the evil effects of liquor drinking.   Along with such assertions put testimony like the following confession of a hard working man arrested recently for homicide :   "I am forty-three years old, have been sixteen years in this country, and have worked at Tiemann's paint factory fifteen years.   I have a wife and three children.   I live on the top floor, and Lippold on the second floor of the same house.   We had some angry talk four weeks ago, since which time I have avoided him and kept up stairs after getting through my day's work so as to keep out of trouble.   On Sunday I went for a walk by the river and when I come home went straight to my room. Afterward I came down in my stockings.   As I came out on the stoop he hit me, and I got mad and stabbed him with my knife.   I did not mean to kill him.   I did not say anything to provoke him before he hit me.   I was not much drunk, I think, having drank only four or five glasses of beer.   I never had any similar trouble before."—The Signal.

And as corroberating evidence read the following :

"In America it is constantly reiterated that in France where everybody uses light wines, no one is ever known to be intoxicated.   It is stated in the Parisian police reports that in the first four months of this year (1882) over 20,000 people were arrested in Paris for drunkenness.   One of these statements is false.   Why don't they punish the police in Paris for falsifying their reports and slandering their city ?"—Golden Censer.

And then as an evidence that the use of everything in the way of intoxicating beverages are on the rapid increase in America, read the following extract :

INCREASE OF BEER DRINKING.—"The consumption of malt liquor in this country has increased over 100 per cent. in ten years.   'During 1880,' says the Retailer, the organ of the brewers, 'taxes were paid on 13,374,000 barrels, or 414,000,000 gallons.'   This is equivalent to about 150 mugs for every man, woman and child in the country.   Leaving out the females and children, this vast quantity represents 600 glasses a year for each male over twenty-one years old in the United States.   At five cents a glass this beer manufacture of 1880 brought $375,000,000 or about $7.50 per capita for every man, woman and child.   This is a quarter more than the total expense of running the United States Government."

What think you of these statistics? intemperance in every form and by every conceivable means on the spread and increase.   The circle of its deadly influence widening as the world moves on its march of progress. Its prevalence is greater to-day than ever known during the history of the race. Upon this point Fanny Kemble Butler says:

"Fifty years ago the abuse of intoxicating liquors or the vice of drunkenness were then unknown in America. The use of either beer or wine at the tables of the Philadelphians when I first lived among them was quite exceptionable." The Quakers were always a more steady and sober people than the Puritans of New England, who would have their rum and cider. Fifty years ago the consumption of whisky was but a drop in the bucket compared with the present day and lager beer was unknown. We had then comparatively no railroads, no telegraphs, no telephones, no steamships, and not many common schools. With the advance of science and great discoveries come hand in hand—a larger consumption of intoxicating liquors, a greater increase of crime, poverty and misery. Our progress in all that constitutes a Nation's greatness has not reduced the quantity of manufactured poisons and the number of prisons and almshouses."

Then away forever with the fatal delusion and misconception that in the event of time intemperance will disappear, that this great problem of the liquor traffic will adjust itself, or that the traffic will become so nicely adjusted to society, that no one will be offended by it. Or away with that still more ensnaring delusion, that milder and more assuasive beverages are to take the place of those fiery, inflaming drinks that work such speedy ruin, destruction and death. All such theories are intentionally deceptive by those who advance them, for intemperance springing from all these fruitful sources, is increasing at a ratio that distances computation. Do not all the facts relating to intemperance, gleaned from every conceivable source, contribute to the theory that legal prohibition is the only possible remedy. If it is admissible, if it is the right and proper thing to do, to reform an evil, manifestly the only proper way to effect such a reformation is to strike at the very heart of the evil, with the view of exterminating it altogether. This is what prohibition aims to do with intemperance. The orthodox temperance reformers have no patience with assuasive and attenuated theories or measures that savors of compromise. And the purified and the universally enlightened Christian civilization of another century will rest contented with nothing less severe than the radical extermination of every means and influence that fosters and promotes intemperance.

Another fallacy that suggests itself to our mind, but one which cannot be classed as a popular fallacy, is the theory advanced, that since most of crime and casualities in large cities are occasioned by the use of liquor, that the license be put at a price that will cover the cost of criminal prosecutions, and all loss of property traceable to this source. And when the license is paid, for the saloons to go ahead with their work of destruction. This would be a capital plan, were it only practical; as the effect would be to speedily, financially bankrupt every capitalist who would have the temerity to engage in the wicked business. But such a theory cannot be reduced to a practical system. To a very limited extent only could such a plan be brought into practical effect. If a man crazed with drink should, through carelessness or viciousness of temper or spirit, set fire to a store or dwelling, the loss sustained might be paid out of the license fund held in reserve for that purpose. But there is a character of losses sustained by the use of strong drink that cannot be estimated in dollars and cents. There are every year losses sustained through the power of liquor that all the gold and silver in the world could not pay. These losses are the murdered victims of the deadly cup, and the weeping and broken hearted fathers, mothers, brothers, sisters, wives and husbands that mournfully file into a funeral procession and follow the hearse, bearing the victim of drink to an ignominious grave. Silver and gold are not adequate to such a loss. There is absolutely no panacea for the bereaved affections of a broken hearted wife or mother, weeping over the dishonored grave of a fallen husband or son. You will search among the treasures of earth in vain for anything adequate as a compensation for the loss of the life of a kindred or companion through the power of drink.

Who could be so base and sordid as to offer money as the compensation of of a bereaved and broken heart. A man is worth a million of dollars. His wife, the bride of his early manhood, lay upon the couch of death arrayed for the grave and the eternal sleep. His heart is crushed with the burden of grief, and as he weeps the tears of sorrow and anguish he utters from his heart's recesses, "I will give up all my treasures if God will but give me back the companion of my life, but all to no avail, and such a thought is but mockery. The same is true when the death angel knocks at the door of the unbroken household and takes away the fair-haired little girl or the prattling bright-eyed boy, the favorite and flower of the garden, the father bends in grief and says, "Oh! that God had taken away my earthly treasures and left me my child," and the weeping mother takes up the refrain and says, "Yes, if we owned all the wealth of the universe we would give it up if we could but have our Annie or Willie back again. Death has robbed us of a priceless posession.' But death under such circumstance as this is much more tolerable than death that comes as a consequence of drink, dissipation, violence and crime. Strong drink murders the bodies and souls of one million of men annually, and ten millions of persons bow their heads at the open graves and weep out of the bitterness and sorrow of a heart that knows no surcease, comfort or hope, and yet in the face of this awful array of statistics men are found who suggest that if a large enough price should be charged for license for drink that this wail of human anguish and woe might be hushed into silence and the sale of liquor proceed unmolested. Here we dismiss this subject of such hidious deformity.

Again we consider briefly another popular fallacy. It is this, the vicious theory is universally advanced, and that with an air of confidence, that if legal prohibition should be enacted that it would be so invasive of personal freedom and individual rights, and so objectionable to the tastes and wishes of the people that such a law could not be enforced or sustained. Or in other words a free country and a free people will not tolerate sumptuary laws. It is enough probably to say that such a theory is revolutionary and nihilistic in its tendency and origin. Such a theory, if put into practice, would result in a revolution. But there is no danger. The wish is father of the idea. Men who love strong drink better than they love the interests of humanity, better than they love domestic happiness, and better than they love their soul, only wish that it might be true, that, if in the event of time, their lives of dissipation and licentiousness should be constrained by a law restricting their sensual liberty, that they might be able to overrule, break down and invalidate such a law.

It is true that putting a law upon the statute books is one thing and enforcing it is quite another. But legal prohibition will cost such a struggle that it will certainly be enforced when once enacted. The same suffrage element that enacts such a law will vigilantly guard its enforcement. It is a bold statement to make that a national or constitutional law enacted by the sovereign will of the American people cannot be enforced. It may be said that nothing is impossible with Americans. Certainly the enforcement of a constitutional law is not one of the impossibilities. It is constantly reiterated by the opposing host that "prohibition will not prohibit." Perhaps it will not, at least the talked of prohibitory law—which yet is scarcely in sight—will not prohibit. But when the much talked of law is once placed upon the statute books, we may be able to talk of its enforcement with a more marked degree of confidence. Most certainly is it true that the assertion that a law enacted by the suffrage element of our people cannot be sustained and enforced is wantonly false and unworthy of respectable notice. Such a vicious theory is unrepublican, and is out of harmony with the spirit of free government. It is the cavil of those to whom liberty means license, and who would, if invested with the power, overturn free institutions. But our Government is abundantly able, and will, if the opportunity presents itself, rebuke and destroy such a sentiment. The majesty of the law will not suffer reproach or violence, and if it be that there is within the State or Nation a power greater than the State or Nation itself, the sooner the discovery is made the better.

The institutions of free government are founded upon the respect of the individual for the laws. Withdraw that respect, and with it the support of the government is withdrawn, and the structure of the Republic falls in ruins. It cannot be that in this country, where freedom is the birthright of the individual, and where a sacred regard for its laws is lodged in the heart of every true citizen, that the legally constituted authorities can fail in the preservation and enforcement of legally enacted laws. It will be a dark day in our country's history when its laws cannot be enforced; when the lawless can rise in their strength and over-ride the will of the American people, and trample beneath their feet constitutional laws and invalidate constitutional amendments. Such a thing in the progress of human events may come to pass. We know not what the future has in store for us, but such a thing will not transpire until the star of Republicanism wanes in its glory and sinks into eternal night behind a clouded sky.

In closing we will consider briefly the fallacy of fallacies or what may be called the prince of fallacies; namely, the tenderly cherished theory that legal prohibition cannot be accomplished. This belief is cherished mainly by those who find comfort in cherishing it. The thought is the vagary or superstition of a darkened understanding and justly belongs to a pagan civilization. No one who is in sympathy with the vital progress of modern times, which is revolutionizing the customs and overturning the theories of the race, or no one who is actively interested and identified with the promotion and upbuilding of Christs kingdom will subscribe to any such antiquated theories. Of course it is not worth while to be dogmatic in the discussion of the ultimate successful adjustant and settlement of this great temperance issue, but be it remembered that faith is the foundation stone in the structure of every successful enterprise or undertaking. The work of any individual or human organization that is not founded in faith is as the fragile reed, uprooted by the storm, or as a cloud without water carried about of winds, or as the raging waves of the sea "foaming out their shame," or as a wandering star drifting in the darkness without a destiny in view.

The only evidence attesting or indicating the ultimate success of the temperance movement worth considering is that temperance is the cause of humanity and of God, and every influence and factor in the affairs of earth that is contributing to the advancement of Christian civilization is also aiding in the solution of this momentous problem. The woes and sorrows of the race is greater than it can bear, and it is the part of wisdom to throw off the burden of intemperance. It can be done if the majesty of the law is involved. Why shall it not be done. Surely the purest and noblest motives actuate the brave and faithful soldiers fighting in this humane and divine cause. The enemies of the temperance movement who assume to know that it can only culminate in defeat, do not look at the end from the beginning. They do not exercise any faith in the triumph of moral principles or the success of an undertaking that has a moral purpose in view. They are fully aware that the whisky business is immoral in every respect and in every aspect, yet they firmly expect to see the business perpetuated, increasing and swelling in magnitude until its accursed power destroys everything that is pure and of good report, and until it fills the earth with woe and misery and crowds hell with perishing souls.

Surely the lines are well drawn, and the field of both is mapped out. Surely it is a warfare of the soldiers of Christ, against the armies of Satan entrenched behind the barricks of hell. It is a campaign that will cost many a weary march, many a sleepless night, many a wounded heart, and many a faithful comrade will fall in death while the contest is still fiercely raging. But courage is the watchword, and where is there a friend of humanity and of God that would not count it gain to give his life to such a cause, even though he should not live to see the day of triumph. The work is of God, yet its accomplishment depends upon human agencies. Effectual systematic work by all who befriend the interests of temperance would speedily bring upon us the day of triumph, when the shout of conquest shall go up from around every camp fire, and the song of victory shall go up from every heart. The temperance movement at the present time demands a marked degree of courage on the part of those who are sustaining the cause. The present is a critical time in its history, for the work is so nearly accomplished, the strength already developed in almost every State in the union is so nearly adequate to the task of overturning the liquor traffic that a courageous advance movement of all the forces of the temperance army would win the victory for which they have been struggling through ages.

Perish forever the stupendous fallacy that prohibition is impracticable or impossible of accomplisnment. Nothing that is worthy of accomplishment is impossible in this age of enterprise and activity. The current of revolution that is bearing upon its bosom the temperance cause is so deep and strong as to bid defiance to those who would resist its sweep or change its course. We are witnessing the era of moral triumph and the resurrection of a fallen race from the grave of lust and sin, and in the sweep of revolutions the interest of Christ and humanity cannot be better subserved than by the destruction of the traffic in liquor. Then let the friends of temperance be steadfast in effort, firm in faith, and grounded in confidence. For there are reasons for encouragement for well directed and untiring effort. Who will argue the contingencies of defeat, or quail in the day of battle? Let us fight on amid perils and against discouragements; and after awhile God will crown his faithful soldiers with triumph, and from the plains and hilltops of our beloved land will ascend shouts of victory that will rend the vaulted heavens. For when we talk of moral triumph do we not remember that it is prophesied that Christ shall come in the glory of the Father and in the clouds of heaven, and in coming destroy wickedness by His presence, and purify by the fire of His breath the moral atmosphere of earth. And if it be true that this prophecy has a spiritual meaning—and that Christ is not coming in person—has not this prophecy a corresponding reality in the work to be accomplished? And is it not true that Christ's kingdom is accomplishing this in its spread from the rising to the setting of the sun? And is it not true that the kingdoms of this earth are fast becoming the kingdoms of our Lord and Savior Jesus Christ? And is not the prophecy being fullfilled, that the knowledge of the Lord shall cover the earth as the waters cover the deep? And is it not true that one of the greatest barriers in the way of wicked men perpetuating the iniquitous business of strong drink, and of every other wicked and immoral practice is the destruction of these prophecies of Divine Revelation—yea, the destruction of the whole Word of God itself? For upon these prophecies the Christian soldier poises his shield, grounds his weapons of warfare, and rests.

Temperance in its Relation to Christian Life.

***

shall speak upon the subject of temperance in its relation to Christian life, or attempt to show that religion is the only safeguard against intemperance, and shall speak in the interest of the individual and not waste the hour by attempting to solve, as if by one stroke the great problem of intemperance, a problem which cannot be solved, or which can only be solved in the ages to come.

Life upon earth with the human race has and ever will be a constant struggle and warfare with animal passions and appetites, and the race will never be freed from this struggle while proned between earth and heaven. Those temptations and allurements of sin that tend to drag men down to ruin, physically and morally, may be modified and to a great extent subdued; but every individual being that is born into this world, has a heart proned to sin as the sparks are to fly upward. Sinning is the normal nature and disposition of fallen man, and if in his early life Satan gets control of him before the influence of religion tempers his heart he will sin in the face of every influence that can be brought to bear.

The right to sin is mans supreme prerogative and that right cannot be legislated away from him, with any degree of success. You may by legislation drive the liquor traffic out of a single State, you may possibly drive it out of the union of States, but you cannot drive it out of the world, and if you suppress by legislation the sinful use of strong drink because it is ruinous to the race; wicked men can devise something equally as ruinous to mankind to take its place. The human heart above all things is deceitful and desperately wicked, and you cannot legislate away its right to be wicked. You may by legislation draw some boundery line that will prevent a man from running in a certain direction headlong to destruction, but he can face about and run to destruction in some other direction; and legislation against the liquor traffic is nothing more or less than a boundery line drawn by the civil authorities to prevent men from plunging over the precipice of ruin and death. Strange as the declaration may seem it is nevertheless true, painfully and sadly true; and if a man by reason of his depraved nature is thus bent on self destruction he will accomplish his willful designs despite legislative interference. It may successfully head him off in one direction but he will turn and go to destruction in another way. If a man has it in his heart to destroy himself he can find a precipice in any direction he may turn. And legislation is a feeble influence and hindrence to prevent a man from sinning or taking his own life, if his heart is set upon that purpose and Satan is back of him prompting him to carry out the bent and inclination of his depraved mind.

I would vote in favor of Legislation against the liquor traffic, if I had half a chance, and expect to see Legislation come up grandly to the assistance of the temperance cause. But at best it is a partial and temporary result or effect, that takes away by the majesty of the law the right of man to sin in one certain direction, when a thousand other directions are open before him or may be opened up. It is a partial and temporary reformation that restrains man by the force of law from the commission of sin and crime, but does not touch his heart and conscience. It is like confining a man within prison walls. It prevents the possibility of the commission of crime, but it does not effect the reformation of the criminal's heart. It is admissible and right. But it is not effectual. So Legislation in its relation to intemperance is perfectly proper and admissible. But I believe God has a better and more effectual way for the reformation of fallen man. If intemperance is suppressed through the influence of legislation, without reforming men's morals, they will most assuredly find some substitute for it, something to take the place of intemperance equally as destructive or debasing. You may not accept this declaration, but it is nevertheless true. This Nation struggled with the question of human slavery for fifty years. Eventually it went down before the mighty clash of arms. Now twenty years later, turn about and look at its twin relic, Polygamy as it stalks with giant strides across the continent. Think you not that when it goes down, too, perhaps before the clash of arms, that Nihilism, or some other foe to civilization, will distress and burden our Nation?

What is the principle involved in legislation against intemperance? It is this: You take away from men their chosen implement of self-destruction, but you leave their hands free to grasp another impliment of a different make and character, and with it they have as much as ever freedom and volition to accomplish their designs. You change the course of the stagnant stream but you do not purify the water. Men with willfully wicked hearts—and a great many have that kind—are like mischievous children. The mother discovers their idle hands engaged in some misdemeanor or work of destruction. She corrects them and sends them away, and they turn in diligent search for something else of a mischevious character that they can do, and not until their hands and feet are tired will they quiet down. Thus men who are evilly inclined will not quiet down until they have run the whole gauntlet of social dissipation and crime. Men with hearts inclined to sin and to evil and destructive practices and vices have a freedom and volition of mind and heart that cannot be restrained or circumscribed by Legislative bounderies or suffrage laws. Even God did not circumscribe the boundery limits within which a man's mind and heart might revel and range at will. He did not manacle the soul and say to man you shall not have the right and liberty to do this or that at will if you choose to do it, but He gave him the freedom He gave the mountain eagle which can soar above the clouds or spread its wings and speed its flight across continent or ocean. Think you then that one half of mankind can bind and fetter or circumscribe the boundery limit of the mind and heart and dispositions and desires of the other half. No they had as well undertake to change the form of constellations in the heaven or reverse the course of the gleaming planets that sweep through space.

Men may think that they have accomplished a great work when they have suppressed intemperance by legislation and may feel proud of what they have done. But this does not reform a man. He still is a free moral agent, and has freedom of will and disposition of heart to continue in sin, and will seek some other course of sin and death. And when he turns to exercise his right, he mocks at the lofty and philanthropic aims and purposes of men to circumscribe the limit of his freedom as a man. No, men love to sin, and because they love to sin, they will not give it up; but will devise ways of sinning and follow in them until they are brought to the knowledge of the adorable God. Mankind, generation after successive generations in this world have got to fight sin and evils in one form or another as long as the world endures. And the sooner men make up their minds to this, the sooner they will arrive at a wise conclusion.

You ask, is this conflict between good and evil never to cease? Is there eventually to be no illustrious victory for those who have bravely fought against the wrong? I answer no, unless Christ should come in the glory of heaven, and destroy wickedness by the brightness of His presence, which he is prophesied to do. For wickedness in this latter age is on the rapid increase, rather than on the decrease. And this also is a prophecy of Divine Revelation. But it is well enough for those who have this work at heart of fighting intemperance to be inspired by the belief, that they will ultimately come off victorious; that by some grand stroke of diplomacy or warfare they will completely crush this foe to the earth, and that after that all will be serene and lovely. I would not break the spell of enchantment if I could. For in the warfare with our enemies we need the inspiration that we are going to come off conquerors, whether we conquer or not.

We might consider moral suasion in its relations to intemperance but we will not take up time by so doing. I will simply state that it is my conviction that this means or influence plays a feeble part in the effectual and substantial reformation of the poor unfortunate drunkard.

You ask if neither local option nor moral suasion are going to work the triumph of the temperance cause, and effect the reformation of the inebriate class of mankind what is going to do it? I will tell you what will do it: Christianizing the world. Bring humanity far and near, wherever it is to be found, to Christ. But this is the course that the temperance workers have well nigh abandoned. But have you never read that the stone the builders refused became the head of the corner, the chief corner stone. Men are not very likely to succeed in reforming and reclaiming fallen men by taking the work out of the hands of God and attempting to accomplish it in their own names and by their own hands "not by might or by power but by My Spirit saith the Lord." Is this divine work of reclaiming fallen man to be accomplished? "Man proposes but God disposes."

    The reclamation of man from the course and career of a drunkard is a work that is divine in its nature and character, its tendency and principal, so much so that it can not be unassociated with God, and cannot be effected independent of God's assistance and co-operation. To reclaim man and put him on the way to heaven is a work so sublime in its very nature and character that it could alone have originated in the mind and heart of God, and this work cannot be accomplished independent of the co-operation of Gods spirit.

If intemperance should be suppressed it should be suppressed because it involves sin, and not merly because it is destructive to human life. The latter reason is a very good reason why it should be suppressed, but it is not the best reason. If you go back far enough you will find that because it is sinful to be intemperate is the best reason why the sweep of intemperance should be stayed if possible. If this then is the valid reason why, then it takes you direct to the throne of God as the source from which all help must come in the struggle that is to win the triumph over this enemy of mankind and of heaven.

Intemperance as a curse and blight upon mankind had its origin and now springs from the depraved condition of man's heart. And we may ask with emphasis, is it possible to remedy this evil and leave man's heart untouched, unchanged and unimproved? I apprehend that God who holds the destiny of men and of the world smiles at the inventions and essays of men to change and direct the order of affairs in this world, especially when they attempt to do such things in their strength and in their own way.

When you come to fathom intemperance, you will find the cause seated down deep in the heart of man, where legislation or any other device of man cannot touch it. And yet men say, by legislation, or by local option, or by moral suasion, we are going to destroy this accursed thing intemperance.

I claim that if by such means intemperance is modified or completely, checked, that the result will be but temporary; that in other years and in other generations this evil passion of man's heart will assert itself, and the battle will be to fight over again. Men that are given to sinful practices and appetites that tend to their destruction, must be reformed at heart. This will save them for time and eternity. And reclamation from the evils of intemperance implies the conversion of a man's soul and a change of heart that touches the profoundest depths of his moral nature. And this is the work of ages to come, and the completion of this task extends to the centuries yet in the future. It will come with the gradual redemption of the world from sin, and through the evangelization of mankind. It is evident that men are in greater haste to redeem the world from intemperance than God is to redeem it from sin in its multiform phases.

It is very natural for men to be philanthropic in their disposition. When men with good hearts look around them and see suffering humanity upon every hand, their hearts very naturally and almost unconsciously gushes out toward them. Although they themselves may not have very great faith in God or be Christians at heart. But it is wisest and safest for those of us who are working for the alleviation of suffering and for the reformation of fallen man, to place our hands as those of little children in the great hand of God, that He may sustain and lead us on to triumph in this divinely instituted work.

If the world is to be saved from drunkenness and the kindred vices and crime that drag men down to death and eternal woe, it must be lifted up to a higher and nobler moral and intellectual plane of life, and the accomplishment of this great work is dependent upon what God by his spirit is willing to do in assisting man. But God can be depended upon for his willingness in this matter.

The true solution of the problem of intemperance is the solution of the problem of every sin and vice to which mankind is heir. The solution is in the improvement of the belief and morals of mankind, and all spasmotic efforts along any other line, by which suffering is to be alleviated and intemperance checked are temporary in their results.

Why are men drunkards? It is because their belief and morals does not raise than above the plane of a drunkards life. It is because they have no aspirations, aims and purposes in life that lifts them above the degrading and debasing sensual appetites of animalism. They have not those conception of true nobility and of a noble life that lifts man up into the realm of thought, and that brings to his mind the inspiration of the higher life and the divine life.

Take a man that is moored altogether to this world, who does not rise in his mind above the things which he handles with his hands and sees with his eyes, who has no conception or thought of heaven and the life beyond, and who has no aspirations in that direction, who is content to grovel among the things of earth and wallow in the mire as does the swine; such a man is the man to make a drunkard out of, and it is not strange that he becomes a drunkard and dies such. For, take life here on earth and strip it of aspirations and hope of the life beyond and of the consolations of religion and it is not worth living. A brute animal may enjoy and no doubt does enjoy life, but man cannot live this life on the plane of animalism and get enough of employment out of it to compensate him for the trouble of living.

Take human life in its relation to earth and earthly things, and it is so fraught with discouragement, hardship, trials and misfortunes that a great many men break down under the burdens of life. They find themselves overcome with the heat and burden of the day, and stand face to face with the issue and question—"Is life worth living?" At this crisis in life a meagre proportion seek refuge and consolation in the arms of Christ, the Divine Savior. But an infinitely larger proportion seek the consolation of the maddening bowl, and from that time dates the beginning of a drunkard's career. Trouble breaks men down in life. They then take to drink to drown their troubles, and they drown themselves and their souls in perdition. Immorality and unbelief lie back of their rash act and fateful course. You may argue this question up one side and down the other from this until the day of doom, and it will ever resolve itself into this—that the lack of faith in the eternal principles of righteousness, justice and truth lies at the foundation of sinning; and leaves without restraint those appetites which when developed makes drunkards out of men.

Now how are you going to break up this state of affairs? Men sin because they love to sin, and because they have a right to sin, if they choose to exercise that right; and what law enacted by men can deprive them of that right? I do not say that such results cannot be accomplished, but when accomplished they are at best but temporary, and such reformation is not true reformation. Men grasp the idea that to die a drunkard is a terrible thing. It is a terrible thing. But I doubt not that God views these things very differently from the way men view them. We say with one accord that a drunkard's life is a wasted life. We call it dissipation. But in what way is it different or worse than an empty and hollow life, the life of one who has never done a stroke of good or a stroke of harm? We shudder at the thought of a man dying a drunkard. But life upon earth without heaven in view amounts comparatively to nothing. The drunkard can only reach perdition. The moderate sinner along any of the avenues of life or the man who simply leads a life of indifference reaches perdition. A man does not have to be a great sinner to be lost in eternal woe. If he does simply nothing he will be lost, if the Bible is true. And a life of indifference so far as time and earth are concerned is as much wasted as if it had been spent in the revel of drunkenness.

Any life is wasted in this world in which the individual does not prepare for heaven, and if finally we are to miss heaven, so far as we are individually concerned, we probably had as well die an inebriate as any other way. Reform a drunkard without converting his soul, and he will go on down to perdition the same as though he had not been reformed. You save him perhaps a few fitful years of life on earth, but what is life on earth worth without heaven in view. View this matter as you will, I have no doubt but that God makes distinctions which we do not make and cannot make.

I am convinced that the future destiny of a man that dies a drunkard, does not differ materially from that of a man who folds his hands and lives in quiet indifference and goes down to the grave with an established reputation for idleness and worthlessness. And this is the kind of a life most men are living. The average human life in this generation is practically a failure, and uncharacterized by results that bless mankind or take the form of treasures laid up in heaven. And while it is commendable to fight intemperance, it should be remembered that it is no more important to reclaim the drunkard and put him on the road to heaven than it is any other class of mankind. And I vow before God and before men, that if you do not associate heaven with the reformation of a drunkard, that the drunkard is not worth reclaiming, and that there is a very broad sense in which it is true that if a man is to miss heaven at last when this fitful season of life is ended, that he had as well live and die a drunkard as any other way.

Enjoyments in this life are counterbalanced by suffering. Its pleasures are offset by pain and sorrow. It is absolutely not worth living unassociated with religion and the hope of heaven. You say that a man ought to be sober and temperate that he may be useful, useful to himself and to his family—if he has one. But there is no high or noble ideal conception of usefulness unassociated with the religion of divine revelation and the thought of God. The golden pavement that leads up from earth to the eternal city of our king is the royal way of usefulness. That sentimental philanthropy or charity that has no higher purpose than the alleviation of suffering humanity here on earth is a mere shadow or type of that higher and nobler charity that seeks the rescue of men because their souls are worth saving for heaven and eternity. This is the gospel idea ; this is the Christ idea, and it is the idea and policy of the church. Strange indeed it is that Christ never made one single arraignment or allusion either to intemperance or to drunkards, except perhaps in his reply to the Pharisees when they challenged that he was a glutton and a wine bibber.

Christ's mission upon earth, and the mission he intended for the Church, was not merely to save any special or particular class of men, but to save the whole world, to save mankind wherever it is to be found, to save it under all circumstances, and in whatever unfortunate plight or condition it may be found. But to-day we find temperance associations—an association doing a work that is religious in its tendency—we find them doing a special and distinct work, and almost wholly unassociated with the Church and with religious organizations of any class or order. And the man who talks or lectures upon temperance does not rank with ministers of the gospel in dignity and in the estimation of men generally. There is no warrant in the Bible for denominationalism, although there is a warrant there for the Church. And I am sure that there is no warrant in the Bible for temperance associations as a divine institution, any more than there is a warrant for Free Masonry; yet temperance associations are largely doing a divine work, and are working for God. But the Church, though unassociated with temperance associations, is working for the cause of temperance. Annually in our country seventy-five thousand drunkards go down to their grave. Tramping closely behind their heels are seventy-five thousand more to follow them the succeeding year, and so on indefinitely, and the great army can scarcely be numbered. But this class are exclusively outside of the Church. The Church has a great army within its fold that can scarcely be numbered. Suppose the Church had not thrown its arms around this great throng of men and women and brought them within its fold, and lifted them up upon the divine and spiritual plane of life, how many do you suppose of the well-nigh countless multitude would to-day have been drunkards, increasing indefinitely the already unnumbered standing army of drunkards in our own land. Look at it in this light, and also in this other light that the Church is grandly supplied with strong, able and brave men who are willing to dare and to do in the rescue of every poor unfortunate inebriate with whom they come in contact. To teach them of the goodness and mercy of God, to reclaim them and to put them on the road to heaven. That man does not live who will do more to reclaim the drunkard than the Christian will do. The idea of the Church, and the Church is right in this, is to exert an influence, widespread, universal and unconditional, that will enlighten and enoble men, and lift them up upon a higher plane of moral and intellectual life, and inspire them with thoughts of the Divine life. The work is expansive and far-reaching, and comprises the true idea of reformation from intemperance and from every other vice and sin that degrades and demoralizes mankind.

And here is the practical point of what I have labored to explain. Intemperance exists chiefly upon the low grounds of immorality, ignorance and unbelief. Lift men to a higher plane and higher grounds of true moral

moral life and you will seperate them from the appetite of strong drink.   But to do this you say is to Christianize the world, and to make men so Christ-like and saintly that they will not drink because it is sinful is a discouraging undertaking.   Yes, truly it is a discouraging undertaking.   It is a slow tedious process, but it is the only true way of reforming fallen man.   Build temperance movements upon this principle and you have a solid foundation.   Trust God for the results and trust heaven for your reward.

The accomplishment of anything worth accomplishing requires a struggle. A man says I want to be rich, but I have not a dollar to begin with, if I had the foundation laid I would make the struggle for a fortune.   But he rests there, and never in his life makes a step of progress in the work of acquiring a fortune, because he could not take a direct cut across lots he would not make the journey at all.   But this is a mistaken policy.   He had better have made the struggle anyway.   It would have been better for him to have worked hard and diligently and saved one or two dollars a week until he had got the foundation laid upon which to build and amass a fortune than to have done nothing about it and to have abandoned the wish and the longing of his heart.

So in the work of reforming the inebriate class we must first of all have a secure and solid foundation laid upon which to build the collossal structure of temperance ; and then we must work faithfully and diligently as if working for a fortune—to carry out and accomplish our designs and purposes and the desires of our heart, to reclaim and rescue fallen men.   The Church has this foundation laid and is accomplishing this work however slow the progress and with whatever breaks between.   It is lifting humanity gradually to a higher plane of moral principle, of moral excellence and moral living ; and in doing this it is lifting men above the plane of intemperance.   The idea of the Church is to reach out and save the whole world, and in saving the whole world to save the drunkard too.   It is making a pitiful out in this work of such infinite magnitude, yet nevertheless, the Church is the grandest institution and in accomplishing the grandest work on earth.   It well-nigh monopolizes the entire work done for humanity, for nineteen-twentieths of the charitable work of the globe is done in the name of Christ.

If the church rescues the world from the curse of intemperance it will do it because the principle or practice of intemperance is sinful rather than for the reason that it inflicts suffering and sorrow upon the race.   The church will reform the drunkard because he is sinning against God rather than because he is sinning against himself and against mankind.   True reformation consists not so much in putting the accursed drink out of the reach of the drunkard as it consists in teaching him to abhor drinking and abstain from it from principle.

The principle involved in drinking makes intemperance a sin and an offense against God, the results makes it a sin and an offense against humanity. We must teach men to abhor drinking from principle, and because it is sinful, wrong and debasing.   The traffic and manufacture of liquor as well as the practice and custom of social drinking must be held up before the eyes of the world as odious, debasing and demoralizing.   Men must be made to feel that it is disgraceful to touch or taste or handle or even smell the hellish stuff, and that the man who does so is damned for this world and for eternity.   That this vicious and criminal indulgence banishes him from the homes of respectable people,here on earth and banishes him from heaven when he comes to die. That this sinful lust for strong drink brands him as an outcast from the homes upon earth and an exile from a home in heaven. Why! because he is a drunkard? No, because he is a social drinker, a moderate toper. Because of his lust for that fiery beverage that is damning to body and to soul. Because he seeks occasion to drink the accursed draught under pretexts and subterfuges which he thinks will strip it of the sting of sin—such as keep it in stock and close at hand to be used freely for the slightest feighned or unfeigned ailments.

I have no patience with the man who discriminates between the moderate drinker and the drunkard, and says one is respectable and right and that the other is disgraceful and sinful. They are both the same. If there is that in strong drink that will damn a man, it will do it because he touches it, or without touching it he even lusts after it, and not because he dies a drunkard. So far as the future destiny of a man is involved I would as soon take the chances of a drunkard as that of the social or moderate drinker - or even that of the man who has a financial interest in the enterprise of manufacturing liquor, or that of the man who votes for or signs a petition to license the drinking hells. "Birds of a feather flocks together," and in the region of hades men of a principle will meet together. Why! if I sanction or believe in drinking socially, moderately or otherwise, even though I should not touch or taste it myself, that belief or principle would send me to a drunkards hell. I tell you it is possible for a man to be a drunkard by principle. Do you remember that nice distinction the Savior made, "Whosoever looketh upon a woman to lust after her hath committed adultery already in his own heart," that the sin of adultery might be committed in the thoughts of the heart. So it is with drinking. The devil furnishes the lurid flaming beverage of hell and whoever touches it or believes in it is a drunkard by principle and is damned because he has the principals of a drunkard. The social drinker, or the home drinker, or the man or woman who stealthily drink when they go into their closet to pray is no different and no better than the confirmed drunkard who staggers upon the verge of an open grave.

Again, the sale of intoxicating liquors is morally wrong, and it is morally wrong to license such a business; and whoever gives his sanction and vote to license such a traffic, is as guilty of the violation of moral principle as the liquor dealer who stands behind the bar and deals out the subtle poison. The inevitable drift and tendency of social drinking is to moral degradation. To teach men that drinking is morally wrong is to reform them. And to do this is to strike at the very heart of some of the social customs of the world. The Theatre with its numerous immoral features and tendencies, the giddy ballroom dance follow in this train, and are schools for immoral teaching and training; you will find but few—comparatively none—among their devotees who oppose drinking from principle.

But the most distressing and formidable of all social customs is the New Year's day banquet. New Year's calling is the infernal innovation and custom of modern society. The custom of spreading the New Year's table with intoxicating drinks for young people is an infamous and infernal temptation and snare. The result of this un-American custom has been to increase largely the great army of wretched inebriates. There is (when viewed from a moral standpoint) involved in this custom of spreading the New Year's table with ardent spirits all the sin, infamy, degradation, shame and crime, that belong to the drunkard's life. The distressing and formidable results of the custom belong as much to those who countenance and encourage it as it does to the victim who, through its influence, commences a career which can result in nothing less than sin, disgrace and death.

It is the principle involved and that prompts one to take a part in such a henious and debasing custom as social drinking that merits unrestrained censure; there is involved in the very act of taking a single glass the principle and cause that necessitates a drunkard's hell. So far as moral principles are involved an occasional social glass brings a man to the level of a drunkard wallowing in the gutter. The differance between the disgrace and infamy is in the degree and not in the quality of the sin or violation of moral and physicial law. There is involved in the act of taking one glass of strong drink all the debasement, sin and infamy that belong to an inebriate's life and death, so far as the principle itself is called into question.

And those who indulge in the custom of setting the accursed drink before their guests in the social retreat or at the New Year's banquet, need reforming as much as the poor delirious inebriate who is reeling upon the highway. What! you say, condemned because I countenance or indulge in this custom once in a year? Yes, I answer, it is the principle involved. It is just the same whether you do this thing once a year or a thousand times once in a year. Whosoever has offended at one point in the law of the gospel of Christ has offended at every point. But you say it is difficult to be perfect in this world of sin and temptation; yes it is just possible that that is true. But I will tell you what you can be perfect in. You can be perfect in your abhorence for drink, for drinking, and for the drunkard. You can cultivate in your heart to perfection distaste and disgust for drinking, and for the principle involved in the accursed thing. There is no excuse for your not being perfect in your total abstinence, and in your teetotal abhorence of drink and drinking people.

I want to emphasize the thought, that the principle involved in drinking liquor is the thing to be abhorred, and that with an eternal abhorrence, for unless this thought is established and emphasized, this subject is scarcely worth discussing, for the principle involved is worse than the thing itself. And I want to emphasize the fact that it is drunkenness to touch or even look upon this thing of strong drink with any other feeling than that of abhorrence. Alcoholic drinks are the fiery beverages of Satan, the Devil, and whoever drinks them belong to him, and it matters not whether they imbibe freely or lightly. It is the principle involved that makes drink sinful. You may say that these are strong assertions; and they are strong assertions; and whether you accept them as true or not, I know this to be true, and it is only putting the same thought I have expressed in different language—I know, that no one who truly loves the Lord Jesus Christ, and shares a blessed communion with him, and are living day by day conscious of that purity of heart that fits them for heaven; I know that no such a person as this will yield to the temptation of strong drink, or resort to the maddening bowl—the beverage of eternal destruction—for consolation or pleasure.

And here again at a different standpoint we draw the line of distinction. If Christians will not drink from the "tempters" cup, then those who do drink are not Christians. This is the most charitable view—to be truthful and honest that can be taken of this subject of drinking. But is there a rescue from this evil of intemperance you ask. Yes there is a rescue for the drunkard who is on his way to perdition, and there is a forgivness for those who by the words of their lips and by their actions have sanctioned and encouraged social drinking, who have put the cup to the stangers lips, and have taken a hand and a share in making drunkards of men; if not literally drunkards then drunkards by principle.

That rescue and that forgivness is in Christ and His sin cleansing blood. The love of a loving Savior is the only influence in heaven or on earth that has the power to rescue, reclaim and save the drunkard and lift him from the defilements of hell to the purity of heaven.

And now, my closing thought is practically and personally for the hearer. Have you a purpose in life? If so, does that purpose ennoble your life? Does that purpose fill your mind and heart to overflowing with such thoughts and conceptions of hope and promise and of destiny that you feel that you cannot afford to sacrifice these things for the drunkard's cup and revel, or jeopardize them by tampering with those influences that are liable to make a drunkard of you? Or, in other words, are you a Christian? Are you trusting in God? Have you accepted Christ as your strength and guide in life? Or are you fighting the battle of life single handed and alone, without a captain, a helmet, a sword or a shield, relying upon your own strength, generalship and diplomacy to win the victory over the world, over Satan and over death? If so, you need not be surprised at some time or other in life to wake up to the awful realization that you have become a drunkard, and are traveling in the drunkard's wake to ruin and to eternal death.

Are you trying to sail your craft upon the tempestuous sea of life, all alone, without a pilot, without a Savior near upon whom you can call to still the waves when they are threatening to overwhelm you? If so, you need not be surprised if upon some dark and weird night, when the fog and the tempest surround you, your vessel crashes upon the shoals of eternal destruction, and you sink beneath the turbulent billows, to rise again no more forever.

How foolish would the pilot be who should attempt to navigate the great ocean without a compass and a chart! And how certain he would be in the night of tempest and storm to wreck his vessel upon the shoals either in mid-ocean or amid the rocks and breakers of the perilous shore. And this is just what is going to happen to every individual person who attempts to make the voyage of life without a chart and a compass. The Bible is man's chart as he goes bounding over the ocean of life to eternity. And the Holy Spirit of God is the compass that points with unerring certainty to the harbor of Heaven, the eternal haven of the soul. And oh! how foolish it would be for you as the pilot of the vessel of life to refuse to avail yourself of this chart and compass. Or, having started upon the voyage of life with them, when the tempest and the storm breaks, and the lurid lightning flashes along the panoply of the black night, to take up this chart and compass and cast them overboard as in the lashing billows.

And that is just what you individually are doing and have done if to-day you are not a Christian and have not accepted Christ. You are trying to pilot your vessel accross the sea of life without a chart and without a compass, and sooner or later you will certain as fate wreck your vessel upon the shoals of intemperance or some other craggy rock in the perilous waters in which you are sailing, and in the night and the tempest you will sink and perish forever.

There are many who have no thought of ever becoming drunkards but they have no security in this matter and no one is safe from the temptations and allurements of the drunkards life who is not a Christian. They have no chart for the future of life upon earth. They know not what unfortunate occurrence or unexpected event in life may turn their feet in the wake of a drunkards life and a drunkards destiny. Are you a drunkard to-day, if so Christ is your only rescue and redemption from a drunkards career and death. Are you sober and temperate today ; if so Christ is your only security and safeguard that you may not become a drunkard at some time in life. If you are not a Christian then you are standing upon the sinking sand, and I pray you to step and step quickly upon the rock Christ Jesus that you may have a solid foundation for your feet that you may be able to withstand the flood-tide of temptation and destruction. Make haste in taking this step, for life is fleeting as the shade and will soon be gone. The moments and hours like spectres vanish from our sight and the days like white-robed priests pass by, and the thought of coming to Christ goes down in death with the heart that cherished it.

Life is a quick voyage across the narrow sea of time, and we are no sooner launched upon its turbulent waters than we touch the farther shore. We are moving swifter than the flight of an eagle to obey the summons of departure that peals forth from the throne of heaven and reverberates throughout the halls of eternity. This summons calls you to prepare for your eternal destiny, and if you are going to obey the summons you must do it quickly and do it now. 'Our faces are toward the setting sun, and we are moving swiftly down the declining path of life, and the shadows lengthen and fall deep and dark around us,' but to the christian this path leads to the realm of eternal day, and by the dawn and twilight of that day shall they first behold the pearly gates of heaven. May God through riches of infinite love bring those to whom these thoughts are addressed to share his hope and prospect.

The Overshadowing Question.

s a Nation of people we are striving for nobler attainments, morally, intellectually, socially and politically. It is a worthy pride and ambition in a people to rise in the scale of morals and intellect. There is such a thing as a blessed discontent with the environments of life. Aspiration is the child of discontentment. That which we have we do not long for. Imagination sees a sight or hears a sound; borne aloft on wings, aspiration seeks a closer communion and contact with these ethereal fairies of a mystic realm. Beings of a purer nature and who inhabit a realm remote from us, perhaps have no longings to spend even an occasional day upon this earth plane, where we must spend the weary lapse of life. But how different our nature from that of those beings whom by faith we behold dwelling in a realm of celestial purity! How gladly would we exchange abodes with them! How the soul of man in its spiritual moods long for freedom from earth restraints. Hsw fain the wish of the soul that loves purity to exchange earth for heaven—to take to itself wings of light and soar amid and beyond the stars.

One of the important lessons that life teaches, and the intellect grasps most easily is, that if we aspire for nobler things we shall be rewarded by their realization. The man who deeply and sincerely aspires for heaven will very likely realize heaven in the realm beyond. Much that is true respecting heaven is true respecting earth, and much that is true respecting individuals is true respecting Nations. Individuals and Nations may alike aspire to elevation of morals and purity of life. Likewise that which degrades individuals degrades Nations. The question may be asked: Is our country being degraded? Yes, as truly as God reigns this is being done. We cannot without alarm, view some of the threatening evils that exist among us. There exists in this country to-day collossal, social and political evils that threaten national existence. The influence of these evils are widening, as the circle of the waves set in motion by storms at sea widen, and we must as a Nation of people in the future aspire to nobler things or eventually sink down into vulgarism, for the evils that this Nation is tolerating and the crimes and local disorders it is fostering will eventually blot out every trace of virtue and morals in social life.

Efforts must be put forth to restrain some of the evils that threaten our Nation, or eventually the day will come when our people will plunge with the maddening velocity of an avalanche down the mountain slope of virtue. The

good in the world must overcome the evil, or the evil in the world will overcome the good. This is not saying which eventually shall triumph. That is
left and open question, but to my mind we are approaching swiftly an upheaval and a crisis in the affairs of the races and Nations of earth. During the
lapse of three score of centuries the history of earth has been that of a conten-
tious, malignant and stubborn conflict and contest between the good and the
evil that is in the world. An interminable struggle for the supremacy of right
power and rule. Is it not time and would it seem strange if in this age of
promise and hope a crisis should come in which the vexed problem as to whether
good or evil shall rule in the affairs of earth, should be settled; a crisis that
may involve the destiny of the race, for this world is swiftly approaching a
millennial reign or else it is swiftly ripening for the day of doom.

It may be argued that the use of such language as this indicates that we
are floundering in an ocean of conjecture and uncertainty. Or the question may
be asked, can it be that after the lapse of six thousand years there is still a
lingering doubt in the minds of the enlightened people of earth to-day as to
whether the good shall triumph over the evil that is in the world or whether
the evil shall triumph over the good that is in the world? I answer as a stu-
dent of prophecy and history that this doubt legitimately exists. There
are those who think that they hold in their hand the golden key that
unlocks the portal of admission to all knowledge. They think that the
Bible is that key. They believe that eventually the religion of revelation
will compass the whole world and dissipate by its burning rays the evil
influences that are in the world. This may be regarded as a good foundation
upon which to build, and yet it may be likened to casting anchor in the sand.
This faith which is tinged with heroism deserves careful and respectful consideration. It is the faith to which the christian world is anchored, if indeed it
be like casting anchor within a mystic vail.

The question is asked, what progress has been made by this means which
bears the impress of Divinity—looking to the conquest of the world? We
reply that it certainly has not yet conquered the evil that is in the world.
Eighteen centuries have elapsed since Christ graced the earth with his presence
and since the Church was established at Antioch. And what have we to-day?
We have but three nominally Christian Nations, and among the numerous and
extensive heathen Nations of earth the Church has established but a few out-
posts. Infidelity in the heart of Christian nations is keeping pace with Christian advancement. Pagan nations are extending their territory and are
increasing their population at a ratio that distances computation. And in the
distant Oriental nations, where, eighteen centuries in the past, lived the Galli-
lean King—the birth-place of Christendom—there stands to-day dotting its
valleys, plains and mountain sides, the Turkish mosques and pagan institutions
of learning. And the great Christian Temple in which Christ gave to the
world his choicest oracles, lies in ashes and smoldering ruins, and His own
people—to whom he came—are found scattered throughout the earth, a universally infidel nation or people.

Despite of all that christianity has done for the world, "the whole creation
groans and travails in pain until now." Despite of the martyrs blood, despite

of missionary zeal, despite the tears and prayers and labor of christians in ages past and present, the fact remains that to-day the great seething masses that populate the earth are infidel and Pagan in belief and profession. The Church has made some progress, and has in the past and is now apparently moving on to the conquest of the world. But the progress is so slow that it cannot be determined whether it will accomplish this end or whether such an expectation is an illusion of hope. Certain it is that prophecy does not lend encouragement to such an expectation. The divine teacher taught that the wheat and the tares should grow together until the end—or the harvest, and upon every prophetic page we find the unmistakable intimation that the latter days of the worlds history are to be days of peril, when evil shall rear aloft its head, menacing and threatening the overthrow and destruction of everything sacred.

But it is not my purpose or desire in this brief lecture to antagonize the well nigh universally, yet doubtless erroneous Christian belief that the church is to either eventually or speedily convert the world and reclaim it from the power and dominion of evil influences. But the object of this lecture is to show that we are living in an age rife with evil influences that menace the very existance of our Nation, to show that while living in an age when the cry of peace and safety greets our ear from every side, that we are in the midst of perils collossal in size, threatening in attitude and malignant in character. What are some of these evils is a question asked. I will name some of them: Intemperance, Gambling, Polygamy, the Social Evil, Nihilism. In round numbers it is safe to estimate that in Christian America there are one million drunkards, one million gamblers, one million polygamists, one million fallen women and one million Nihilists. An army of five million men and women, the avowed enemies of everything that is good in our Christian land, add to them five million more who would join this army in a crisis hour in the countrys history, and you have an army of ten million men and women, nearly one half the adult population of this country—foes to its best interests and enemies to the good that is in it. An army so great, so malignant and so fierce that should it marshall its whole strength it might destroy with one stroke free government, civil liberty and religious tolerance. It is not so much a foreign foe we need to fear as a Nation as it is foes within. It is not so much invasion by a foreign army we need to dread as it is the uprising and malignant assault of this united enemy who challenge the existence of righteous government and civil liberty.

Intemperance—The Overshadowing Question—is the question which we are to briefly consider at this time. Perhaps this evil, more than all other evils, hinders the progress and challenges the safety of free institutions. It is hydra-headed, and threatens every interest that is sacred to a Christian people and a virtuous nation. It is doing a deep and quiet work, yet its work of desolation is being done with a marked certainty and completeness. It is an organized army accomplishing a work of destruction, and while it does not march with a sounding tread, and to the bugle's blast, and while we do not hear the cannonading, the shock of arms, and the storm of battle, yet it is with dread certainty silently cutting down its million victims annually in the earth.

This terrible, aggressive, advancing, desolating evil is the dynamite influence of the age. Its tendency and aim is the upheaval, destruction and debasement of everything that is good in the world. It is the breath of the Siroco winds that carry with them desolation and death. It is the "serpent" whose touch is death.

The American saloon and the American home, in their relation to each other threaten each other's destruction. The hand of the saloon is against the home, and the hand of the home is against the saloon. The American saloon has made more invasions and destroyed more victims in the American home than all the wars, pestilences and famines that have ever visited our shores. It has plucked the fairest of the land with which to sate it avarice. It has made the wide world a burial-place for its victims. And yet it asks for more. Yet it will not voluntarily loose its venomous fangs from the American home. And it is because of its uncontrollable avarice that the saloon is a menace to Christian civilization and to free government. It claims the whole earth, and would sweep the whole race into the vortex of death. Such is–feebly expressed–the dark and damning character of the American saloon in its relation to the American home, in its relation to Christian civilization, and in its relation to republican government. Some one may say we are painting a dark picture and holding it up to the gaze of the world. But the picture is not overdrawn. It is impossible to paint a picture of the desolating work of the drinking saloon without heavy shadows and a dark background. One cannot, without mingled fear and dread, look upon Michael Angelos' painting of the Infernal Abyss; but that painting, with its deep shadows, its shooting flames, its lurid background, its writhing demons in the torment of unquenchable fire, does not in its terrible revolting character surpass what might be put upon canvass as a faithful and just exhibition of the carnival of blight, of desolation and of death wrought in the rum haunts of our land to-day. Two such pictures, in many of their corresponding, revolting features, would be faithful and undistinguishable counterparts.

Beyond what has been said is this other fact, namely, the distilling, importation, sale and use of strong drink is steadily and swiftly increasing. This is the most distressing and alarming feature of the case. If this work of destruction was decreasing, or were it at a standstill, there would not be the severe necessity of taking immediate steps looking to the abolition of the whisky traffic by legal prohibition. It is threatening the destruction of the Nation, and the Christian people of this country have got to pummel and crush this stone, or this stone will fall upon them and destroy them. There are seventy-five thousand people drinking themselves to death in this country every year. In ten years from now the army of drunkards who perish annually will number one hundred thousand and so on ad libertim infinitim.

But if I have overdrawn the picture of the ravages and destruction wrought by the American saloon, others have done the same. I am not too selfish to share with others in this address the opportunity of speaking their sentiments. Let us see if they do not likewise characterize the whisky traffic as the overshadowing question in this country.

INTEMPERANCE IMPEACHED.—Dr. Chalmers arraigned intemperance in the following words: "Before God and man, before the church, the world, I impeach intemperance. I charge it with the murder of innumerable souls. I charge it as the cause of almost all the poverty, and almost all the crime, and almost all the ignorance, and almost all irreligion that disgrace and afflict the land. I do in my conscience believe that these intoxicating stimulants have sunk into perdition more men and women than found a grave in the deluge which swept over the highest hill-tops, engulfing the world, of which but eight were saved. As compared with other vices, it may be said of this, "Saul hath slain his thousands, but this David his ten thousands.'"

Some paper says: "Liquor is a little demon, but mighty in its power. It does not fill up the glass, and yet it fills a Nation with untold woe. It is only a ripple on the waters of life; and yet one drop of its spray penetrates the soul, as quicksilver penetrates a rock. It dries the well spring of a generous nature, and withers all the attributes of manhood."

Joseph Medill's conclusion on the labor question is: "The waste of earnings on drink leaves the wage workers poor, and poverty renders them discontented. The reform most needed is temperance."

"Let moderate drinkers know that light wines pave the way for whisky and rum; and moderate drinking for drunkenness, disease and death."

"What is my opinion of intemperance? It is a fire we kindle in ourselves, without a dollar's worth of insurance on the premises."—Mrs. Brown in Merchant Traveler.

Intemperance in its relation to crime: Emory Storrs says "the 4,000 saloons in Chicago bear the same relation to the penitentiary that the Sunday-schools do to the church."

The Grand Jury of St. Louis have made a report in which they say 80 per cent. of the crime and pauperism of the city is directly traceable to the saloons, and recommend the minimum license for liquor-shops be put at $1,000 and those selling beer and wine only $500.

Rev. Dr. Kittredge says: "There are 3,100 saloons in Chicago, or one to every 193 of our people. The money spent for liquor in this city last year was $15,000,000. There were 18,000 arrested for drunkenness last year, one-half of all the arrests made. There were 8,000 girls and women arrested in 1883. Over 6,000 of the arrests were below the age of 20. Think of this ye women who sit here in your cushion, under the soft glow of these many lights, and listening to our sweet music."

Its work abroad:

"The Union Signal" says: "An English gentleman, with a faith in hard, unromantic statistics, has carefully studied the causes of pauperism among 254 cases sheltered by the workhouses of Manchester. Old age, he found, had brought thither nearly one-eighth; disease and accident one-seventh; idleness, free from drink or crime, NOT A CASE; drunkenness in men, one-fourth; drunkenness in women, one-twentieth. The widows and children of drunkards numbered one-fifth of all paupers. And the cold proof from these facts is that the liquor traffic breeds fifty-two per cent. of the pauperism of Manchester. It is probable that similar investigation in this country would not show any less activity in beer and whisky as producing agents? Who says that saloons add nothing to the country?"

"Statistics show that in Denmark, whose male population succeeds in drinking annually fourteen gallons of spirits per capita, drunkenness has to do with thirty-one per cent. of the serious and sixty-one per cent. of the petty crimes committed."

The relation of drinking to murder in the State of Kentucky. A review of the murders committed, springing from the free use of strong drink:

Transcript: "The sheriff and a prominent physician of Whitley county says that 'shooting was as common as dancing in his county. Within the last twelve months thirty-nine deaths have occurred from pistol shots, and the fortieth one is now supposed to be on his deathbed."

Herald Enterprise: Since March 1865—a period of about eighteen years—fifty-five murders have been committed in Logan county; fifty-five persons have been arraigned and tried by our courts for the crime of homicide, and of all that number not a solitary offender has been hanged by law; only two have been adjudged to serve for life in the penitentiary, and one of them was recently restored to the bosom of his country by the misguided clemency of the late Governor of Kentucky. This record is simply appalling. One would naturally suppose that most of this bloody history was written immediately after the war—at a time when the shadow of that great tragedy spread its face over the hearts and minds of men, when memories of battle fields and brutal deeds blunted the sensibilities and taught mankind to scoff at the sanctity of human life. But, unhappily, such is not the case. In 1865 only one murder was perpetrated. In 1866 only two, while in the year 1881 seven men "died with their boots on" in our midst, and eight heroes of the pistol and stiletto have already triumphantly swung the scalps of their victims to their belts in the year 1883. This is official history—copied from the files of the office of the Clerk of the Logan Circuit Court.

THE ENORMOUS COST OF DRINKING.—The drink bill of the Nation is in round numbers, one billion dollars annually.

A careful calculation shows that $2,000,000 worth of alcoholic drinks are used each day in this country.

Pennsylvania receives an annual income of $76,000,000 from her mineral wealth, but spends it all and $2,000,000 more, for her annual liquor bill.

"The Anvil" says: "Intoxication costs the United States annually one thousand millions of treasure. It costs one hundred thousand lives. It produces seven-eighths of the crime and pauperism in the country. It causes nine-tenths of the ignorance and illiteracy. It is indirectly the cause of nearly all the carelessness which results in accidents destructive of life and property. As a consequence life insurance companies are refusing to take risks on habitual drinkers. Fire companies are declining to insure saloons and restaurants as extra hazardous. Railway companies are discharging all conductors, engineers, and brakesmen who drink. Steamboat owners are requiring their officers to abstain from drink when on duty. Why do you not vote as these men act? Acts are prayers."

The enormous amount of money spent for liquor in the United States may be more clearly realized when compared with other expenditures which are estimated by the Union, such as $505,000,000 for bread, and $303,000,000 for meat, showing that more is paid out for liquor than for bread and meat together; $290,000,000 for iron and steel, $237,000,000 for woolen goods, $233,-000,000 for sawed lumber, $210,000,000 for cotton goods, $196,000,000 for boots and shoes, $155,000,000 for sugar and molasses, $85,000,000 for public education, and $5,500,000 for missions. This expenditure is only the direct cost. It does not represent the cost of pauperism, idiocy, insanity and crime which are entailed upon the country by liquor.—Chicago Tribune.

DOES WHISKY KILL?—A liquor seller presented his bill to the executor of a deceased customer's estate asking, "Do you wish my bill sworn to?" "No," said the executor, "the death of the deceased is sufficient evidence that he had the liquor."

Dr. Herman Kerr, a celebrated statistician, says that the annual mortality from intemperance in Great Brittain is 40,500.

The most accurate statistics that can be acquired show that in this coun-75,000 people die from the excessive use of strong drink, and at their heels is heard the dismal tramp of an army of 300,000 more drunkards.

The supply on hand:

The Boston Post (Democratic) says: "There are 80,000,000 gallons of whisky in warehouses in the United States, a gain of 73,000,000, in eleven years. There will be enough on hand to enable the Democracy to fittingly celebrate their victory in 1884."

Lexington Press: "The product of Kentucky whisky closing June 30 will be about one-fourth as much as that of the preceding year. The amount manufactured in Kentucky during the year will aggregate about 7,000,000 gallons. The consumption is about 12,000,000 gallons."

KENTUCKY'S LEADING INTEREST.—Production of Whisky and an Estimate of the Number of Drunks, etc.—A Frankfort dispatch of November 23, says: "Some interesting figures are obtainable from the reports of whisky made to the State Auditor for taxation. To October, 1882, there were in bond in the United States 1,313,440 barrels, and of this amount to June 1, 1883, there was only drawn out of bond a little more than 190,000 barrels. Estimating the quantity left for the State's use, and computing each barrel at forty gallons, and it is found there are 44,937,000 gallons left. There are but few "topers" in Frankfort, and from these few it is learned that each gallon will average about sixty drinks. Some assert there are five drinks to each drunk for every ordinary man, but that the average is ten drinks to a drunk for the Kentuckians. Based, therefore, on the latter estimate, which is that of Col. H. M. McCarty, it is amazing to learn that material enough is yet on hand to give Kentucky 260,625,000 genuine corn juice drunks—costing the drinker (say at ten cents a drink, as sold at retail,) $26,962,500, not including the wear and tear of the system, the bruised and bloody noses, the thefts, arson, murder and crimes of all kinds against man and nature, filling hospitals, prisons and poor-houses and destroying the peace and happiness of all social and governmental relations."

Does intemperance affect elections:

CAMPAIGN EVILS.—The St. Louis correspondent of the Advance, wrote to that paper before election as follows: "We are about to have an election in this city, and as our leading daily well say: 'If ever there was an argument for prohibition we have it in the conduct of our politicians.' They are so anxious to prove that they are not temperance men, that some of them resort to a practical demonstration of the fact on the rostrum or street corners. The chief rivalry is in getting low enough down in the dirt before the rum traffic. The supremacy of the liquor interest is absolute, and the question which is facing every citizen is whether we are to let this thing go on, or band together in the strength of righteousness and overthrow this and some other crying evils. It is plain that there is a deep undercurrent of sentiment which would make an organized effort at good government, including a suppression of whiskyism, retrenchment and civil service reform, a mighty success in 1884. The feeling of most good people here in St. Louis, if not throughout the whole country this year, is, that there is much to vote against but almost nothing to vote for.

The character of its work:

THE TRUE PROHIBITION IDEA.—For fifty years Christians and social reformers have been trying to subdue the terrible evil of drunkenness. For half a century preachers and orators have talked, argued and reasoned against the sin, but apparently without much impression being made. The scourge exists just as much as ever, perhaps its effects are greater than they used to be. The gallows is erected, and men forfeit their lives through the inflaming influence of alcohol; the prisons are crowded, the penitentiaries and poorhouses have difficulty to find room for those who have forfeited their liberty through the greatest destroyer of human happiness ever invented.

Inconsistency of license:

"To license shops that beget murder, and then to punish the murder that the State itself has begotten, is indefensible from a moral point of view."

"If drunkenness be the necessary consequence of drinking alcohol it is no use punishing the man who sells the drink, for he is only exercising a business made legitimate by legislation. It is no use stopping, or, rather, attempting to stop, the sale of rum and whisky whilst the National Government licences and receives a revenue from the manufacture of what Dr. Cheever called, 'Distilled damnation.' "

Does Prohibition prohibit?

Jas. G. Blaine says: "Intemperance has steadilly decreased in the State since the first enactment of the Prohibitory law, until now it can be said with truth that there is no equal number of people in the Anglo-Saxon world among whom so small amount of intoxicating liquor is consumed as among the 650,000 inhabitants of Maine."

And yet there are those who call prohibition a phantom and prohibitionists fanatics. But we regard him as the fanatic who blindly, in the face of such facts as the above, holds on to a system that is daily slaying its thousands.

The "Maine Law," prohibiting the manufacture and sale of intoxicating liquors passed the Legislature of that State May 31, 1857, by a vote of 86 to 40 in the House of Representatives. On February 8, 1883, the constitutional amendment prohibiting the manufacture and sale was passed by a vote of 104 to 37. Notice the fact that the people of Maine have tried the policy of prohibition for twenty-five years, nearly a whole generation, and are so well satisfied with it that to-day no opposition can be organized to constitutional prohibition. The results are satisfactory, whatever is said to the contrary.—Independent.

Are certain political parties enemies to prohibition?

Associated Press, September, 1883.—The Kansas Democratic State Convention to-day resolved that the prohibition law is a disastrous failure, and demanded its repeal and the substitution of a license law rigidly enforced.

Is it indeed an overshadowing question.

New York Tribune: It has been said that the end and the test of good government is the greatest happiness to the greatest number. If this be true it must be owned that no Government extant is satisfactorily conducted. For observation shows that, as a rule, political energy is expended upon secondary concerns, while politicians employ all their dexterity in avoiding action upon the great problems which most deeply involve the destinies of the masses. There is to-day in the English-speaking countries no such tremendous, far-reaching, vital question as that of drunkenness. In its implications and effects it overshadows everything else. It is impossible to examine any subject connected with the progress, the civilization, the physical well-being, the religious condition of the masses, without encountering the monstrous evil.

It lies at the center of all social and political mischief. It paralyzes energies in every direction. It neutralizes educational agencies. It silences the voice of religion. It baffles penal reform. It obstructs political reform. It rears aloft a mass of evilly inspired power which at every salient point threatens social and national advance; which gives to Ignorance and Vice a greater potency than Intelligence and Virtue can command; which deprives the poor of the advantages of modern progress; which debauches and degrades millions brutalizing and saddening them below the plane of healthy savagery, and filling the centers of population with creatures whose condition almost excuses the immorality which renders them dangerous to their generation.

New York Tribune: "All these evils, all this mischief, all this destruction of human souls and intellects, go on among us daily and hourly. There are none so ignorant and inattentive as not to have personal experience of some of them; some hearth darkened; some family scattered; some loving heart broken; some promising career ruined; some deed of shame done. Yet how hard it is to get this gigantic evil attacked seriously. Temperance organizations have indeed been fighting it for years; yet popular inertia has resisted their utmost efforts. But has all been done that might and should have been done by the organized agencies that represent the higher life? What are doctrinal points, for example, compared to this ever-present, ever-active, insidious influence? What are sectarian differences by the side of this National curse? Can the churches fold their hands and flatter themselves that their duties are all fulfilled, while the masses prefer the saloon to the pulpit, and while rum rules in politics and society? Are the higher educational agencies doing all in their power to advance civilization while they ignore this obstacle

to progress? Can any political organization be said to represent the best aspirations and the strongest needs of the people, while this abiding source of
misery and crime and poverty is allowed to spread and flourish?

"There is needed something of that sacred fire which kindled into inex-
tinguishable heat the zeal of the Abolitionists, which compelled the abandon-
ment of human slavery, to rouse the National indignation and abhorrence
against this much greater evil. Nothing short of this, it is to be feared, will
impel time-serving politicians to approach, in a spirit of earnestness a subject
which is distasteful to them mainly because they think they cannot afford to
do without the help and support of the class who derive from the degradation
of the foolish and ignorant the means whereby they continue to rule and
plunder those whose sagacity is proof against their snares."

I have thus far set forth a few only of the dark chapters in the awful category of criminal drink, and again suggest that rum drinking is the overshadowing question in Christian America, not only of America but the sin
of intemperance reaches to other lands, and its deep shadow with massive
columns of impenetrable blackness is covering the whole face of the earth.
Fifty years ago the destroying consequences of strong drink was not thought
of in this country. To-day the deep shadow of intemperance has settled
upon the land as a pall. If the evil is not destroyed it will eventually eclipse
the world in deepest gloom. This is not a fancy or illusion but a serious, solemn and awfully impressive truth. Read the history of the rapid increase
and spread of drunkenness in America and you will be convinced that this is
the serious sober second thought of the temperance people. You ask what is
to be done? I answer extermination. You answer, respectable people patronize the liquor saloon and for that reason no attempt should be made to destroy
the drinking saloon. There may be a plausibility in this argument, but the
trouble is we cannot permit the liquor saloon without permitting its consequences. We cannot have the drinking saloon without having the dark
and damning category of crime and casualties that is the sequence of it.

You ask, how is the extermination of the liquor traffic to be accomplished?
I answer by the strong arm of a constitutional law passed and sustained by the
ballot in the hands of a Nation of Sovereigns. You ask what are the prospects of such an accomplishment? I answer the prospects are bright enough
to encourage persistent and unfailing efforts. A grand army of grand men
are in the field, and if they do not conquer they will perish in the battle. The
very sacredness of the cause nerves the soldier for the conflict and for the conquest. Who would not fight in the temperance army when such a warfare
means the protection of home, the reclamation of the fallen and the salvation
of everliving souls. What work on earth is grander? Rescuing fallen man
and putting him on the way to heaven is a work that angels might gladly do.
There is a grandeur and beauty about such a sentiment and such a work calculated to electrify the thinking world.

Too high an estimate cannot be placed upon the exalted character of
temperance work. It is a work that a King might descend from his throne to
do. And the grandest woman in this world is the one who with jewelled
hands reaches down to the filth of the gutter to lift up a fallen drunkard. It

is a work that the Church might gladly do. But the crowning shame of the Church to-day is that as an organized denominational or ecclesiastical body it will not condescend to do this noble work. And enthusiastic, aggressive temperance workers receive but little encouragement from the ministry. Ministers will not preach temperance from the pulpit, because it is not considered respectable—at least not quite elegant to do so. Pharisaic-like they have eliminated the human element from religion. In this age the gospel, in the main, is preached only to the most respectable people, and that in the most respectable way. What a dainty thing the gospel has become in the hands of the ministers of this age. Those who need it most, the poor, the fallen, the outcast, are virtually robbed of their share. And right here is a great danger both to the Church and to humanity. 'We are liable to have the very foundation of the Christian religion to perish beneath us, because we will not, in the spirit of the Master, preach the gospel in its justice, humanity and loveliness to the poor, the oppressed, and the fallen.'

Notwithstanding these discouragements, the grand work of temperance reform goes on. The cause that stands between the Church and the world; the cause that stands between the sacred home and the rum saloon; the cause that stands between the saved and the lost—between heaven and hell—has its champions and invincible soldiers. It is a cause as old as humanity, and has through all the ages been sustained by heroism. And to-day it requires the chivalry and heroism of the soldier at the cannon's mouth to fight against this foe which threatens the very life of our Nation. To fight within the ranks of the temperance army requires something more than mere Christianity as a preparation or equipment. It requires the faith, the chivalry, and courage of the Christian soldier. It requires a love for humanity deeper than mere impulse. It requires a love for humanity as deep as the emotions of the soul. It requires something deeper than the mere desire to do good. It requires a consecration of purpose and of life that blends indissolubly and imperceptibly the finite with the Infinite Character. Clearly evident to all the world must be the fact that there is required of the Christian temperance soldier an aggressiveness and dauntless courage, that is not required of the formal Christian in the work of the Church.

If the dark shadow of intemperance which is hovering over our land, is ever riven and scattered, it will be only when the world awakes to some of its perils; it will be only when christians everywhere shall have put on the whole armour of God, and have confronted the enemy, wearing the breastplate of righteousness and bearing the shield of faith with which to hurl back their missiles of death and ward off the thrusts of their glittering sword. It will be only when every individual christian man shall have acquired the courage to do his share as a soldier and hero in the cause. Every man and woman who feels an interest in the moral elevation of the race long for the enactment of legal prohibition as a restraint to drunkenness in our land. But it is not enough that we desire a thing, we must strive for its attainment and accomplishment. And not until the whole christian world shall move as with one impulse will they ever come off victorious in the cause of temperance. For the cause will triumph only when the religious conscience, as well as the political conscience of the world shall have been aroused and alarmed.

It will require a political and moral revolution and reformation reaching to the ends of the earth to rescue and redeem mankind from the curse of drunkenness. It will take a new and more vital, moral and religious impulse than the Christian world has to-day to grappple with and destroy the demon of intemperance, or to speak very plain, we must have better Christians—more sacrificing and unselfish—and more of them than we have to-day before we will by moral influence or by legal enactment be able to banish the whisky traffic of this country from within its borders, and reclaim a Nation of people from the scourge of drunkenness. We had as well expect to set a pyramid on its apex as to expect to pass prohibitory laws and enforce them in a land where selfishness, greed, avarice and love of money rules in the hearts of men, and where God is defied and the sanctity of the Sabbath is trampled under foot. Not until holiness of life becomes more prevalent, can legal prohibition be enacted and enforced in America.

To what depths of woe, crime, drunkenness and degradation has our Nation sunken when we rightly review and estimate the real character of American citizens. We must call a halt in the career of crime and drunkenness and in our downward course, or else it is a matter of destiny that we must land at the foot of the proclivlous descent of social virtue and morality. To my mind we are—as a Nation of people speeding with the velocity of an avalanche down the mountain slope of virtue and morality. The Christian world needs a new "reformation."

A writer has graced the literature of this century with the following beautiful thought which aptly illustrates the thought I would fain give to the world:

"The Church of Christ, when first founded by the apostles, resembled a pillar of pure, spotless marble; but by degrees the Romish Church succeeded in driving a nail into this marble, once so fair and undefiled, and she used this nail to hang on it a priestly robe, then another, and many more nails were added, on which were placed miters and rosaries, images and amulets, and finally a triple crown towering above the rest. Thus the whole pillar was covered, and the people entirely lost sight of it. They saw only the hangings and forgot the building which they served to conceal. But God raised up the courogeous reformers and made them strong to pluck out these nails and pull down what was suspended to them, and thus the pillar of the truth was once more made manifest to a wondering world."

As Romanism thus obscured the marble pillars in the temple of religion, so has the sin and crime of intemperance within the last half century obscured the lofty ideal once entertained of a people and Nation freed from vice, crime and drunkenness. As priestcraft vailed the face of religion, so has intemperance, within the last century vailed the face of Christian civilization and draped the memory of better days in the past in deepest mourning. The civil war gave a paralytic stroke to virtue and morality in this country, from which it has not yet recovered. And not until the morning of a new reformation breaks in splendor and triumph upon the world will our Nation of people be lifted up from out of the degradation into which it has fallen. Sloth and

popular inertia have the world in their clutches. And not until a new reformation beigns will the mists that hide the face of religion to-day and the gloom
that drapes the memory of our history in the past be dispelled.

I am not saying that religion has not made some conquests, but rather that
sin has made more. I am not saying that religion is a failure, but rather
that, if it does not receive a new impetus and power, in the near future it will
not prove a match for the evil influences that have sprung up in this age, and
which threaten our Nation's existence. Despite of religion, intemperance moves
on at a speed that distances every means or influence by or through which an
attempt has been made to check its sweeping tide of ruin. If the Church or
if religion has the power to save our Nation from drunkenness, it is not using
that power. If there is a means or influence in this country by or through which
our Nation may be saved from the grave of intemperance, it has not yet been
brought into play. The sages and savants of this age would scout the idea
that our Nation of people is sinking into the mire of intemperance and into
the vortex of infamy. But this fact stands well attested, that, if intemperance
remains unchecked and undisturbed by Legislative measures, within one more
decade, half of the wealth of this grand Nation will be absorbed in the vile
liquor traffic, which already is so great as to burden and freight our Nation
with woes and sorrows unbearable.

Our rescue from the curse of intemperance cannot come too soon. If
unduly delayed it may never be accomplished. For the circle of its influence
is widening with the flight of years. For each rising and setting of the sun
witnesses an augmentation of its power. Generations live and perish from off
the earth, yet the evil of intemperance does not abate. But rather the channel of its deadly influence deepens and widens with the lapse of ages. Let
Christian people in our land and in every land unitedly resist the dread evil
of intemperance, ere God smites the world with a curse.

CONTENTS.

www.ingramcontent.com/pod-product-compliance
Lightning Source LLC
Chambersburg PA
CBHW030555270326
41927CB00007B/925